The Kingfisher
BOOK OF
1001
QUESTIONS & ANSWERS
ANIMALS

MICHELE STAPLE & LINDA GAMLIN

KINGFISHER BOOKS

CONTENTS

Kingfisher Books, Grisewood and Dempsey Ltd, Elsley House, 24–30 Great Titchfield Street, London W1P 7AD

First published in 1990 by Kingfisher Books

Reprinted 1990

Copyright © Grisewood and Dempsey 1990

British Library Cataloguing in Publication Data
Staple Michele
  Animals.
  1. Animals.
  I. Title II. Series
  591

ISBN 0-86272-506-2

Edited by Thomas Keegan
Cover Design: The Pinpoint Design Company
Cover illustration: Bob Bampton
Phototypeset by Southern Positives and Negatives (SPAN), Lingfield, Surrey
Printed in Italy

THE ANIMAL KINGDOM

What makes an animal different from a plant?

The main difference is that animals have to eat. Plants can make their own food using sunlight and a green substance in their leaves, called chlorophyll. Animals do not have chlorophyll, so they have to get their food by eating things. Unlike plants, most animals can also move around. But not all animals can move. Some, like corals and sponges, are rooted to the spot for life. Many animals have specialized sense organs such as eyes and ears, which record what is happening around them. They also have nerve cells which carry messages around their bodies very quickly, so that they can react fast.

How does an animal move about?

An animal moves by using its muscles. Muscles are special parts of the body that can contract and shorten, then relax and lengthen again. In most animals, they work by pulling against a hard part of the body, called the skeleton. The skeleton has joints in it, which are flexible, but the joints can only move in certain directions. So the skeleton helps to direct and control the movements of the muscles.

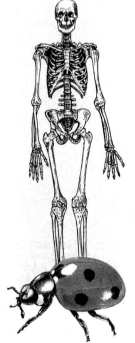

Human and insect skeletons

What is the most important difference between a dog and a spider?

A spider has twice as many legs as a dog, but there is a more important difference concerning their skeleton. A dog's skeleton is made up of long, thin bones *inside* its body. A spider's skeleton is on the *outside* of its body, just like a suit of armour. Insects and crabs have this sort of skeleton too, called an *exoskeleton*. Birds and mammals, such as ourselves, have a skeleton on the inside, called an *endoskeleton*.

What is a vertebrate?

A *vertebrate* is an animal like a dog that has a spinal, or vertebral column. The spinal column is a hollow tube of bone. It has all the most important nerves inside it, running to and from the brain and all the other bones connect up to it. There are five groups of vertebrates: fish, amphibians (frogs and toads), reptiles (snakes and lizards), birds and mammals. All other animals are called *invertebrates*.

How many legs does a land-living vertebrate have?

The usual number of legs in all land vertebrates is four, but some vertebrates have just two, or none at all. Snakes, whales and dolphins, and a group of amphibians called *caecilians*, have all lost their legs entirely. But by looking at their skeletons, we can see that they are descended from ancestors with four legs. In many vertebrates some of the legs have developed into other types of limbs. In birds, the front limbs have become wings. In seals and whales, the front legs have evolved into flippers for swimming.

How many different kinds of animals fly?

Three: birds, bats and flying insects. There was one other group of flying animals in the past, the *pterosaurs* or *pterodactyls*. They were reptiles but they are all extinct now. There are also animals that glide rather than fly. They can travel a long way like this, but they don't flap their wings as true fliers do. Gliding animals include the flying squirrels, the flying lemurs, a flying lizard and even a flying frog. They all have large flaps of skin that help them to glide slowly down.

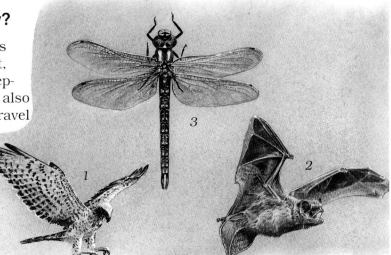

Three types of flying animal: 1. birds, 2. bats and 3. insects

What is a predator?

A predator is an animal that lives by killing and feeding on other animals. The animals it hunts are its *prey*.

What is a species?

A species is the smallest group of animals which are able to breed among themselves but not with members of another species. Their offspring must also be able to breed successfully. Members of the same species usually look very similar. Human beings are all members of the species *Homo sapiens*.

Leopards are sophisticated hunters.

Why do animals breathe?

Animals breathe because they need a gas called *oxygen* which is in the air all around us. There is also oxygen dissolved in water; fish and other underwater animals survive by breathing it. Sometimes water loses all its oxygen, and then the animals in it die.

Which animals live on the nectar produced by flowers?

Several groups of animal live on nectar, the best known are flying insects such as butterflies, moths, bees and hoverflies. In the tropics, some bats live on nectar as well as eating the pollen produced by flowers. There are also various birds that sip nectar, including the sunbirds of Africa and the hummingbirds of the Americas. These birds supplement their diet by eating the insects that they find in the flowers. Finally, there is a small mammal in Australia known as the Honey Possum that takes nectar and pollen from large flowers.

What is a carnivore?

An animal that eats other animals. Animals that eat plants are called *herbivores*. Those that eat all sorts of different food, as we do, are called *omnivores*.

Which animals can change colour instantly?

Chameleons are the best known animals for quick colour changes, but various fish, such as plaice, and molluscs, such as cuttlefish, can also change colour at a moment's notice. All these animals have sacs of pigment in their skin which can expand or contract to produce a different skin colour. They change colour to blend in with their surroundings, or when they are frightened. Cuttlefish can make their bodies pulse with bands of colour to warn off a predator. Flatfish such as plaice just change colour for camouflage, to blend in with the seabed where they are resting.

Which animals give birth to live young?

Mammals – animals such as dogs, cats, monkeys and kangaroos – are the main group of animals to do this. But many other animals give birth to live young as well, including some fish, snakes, insects and starfish. These species are all 'exceptions to the rule' because they belong to groups of animals that normally lay eggs. In the course of evolution, these species have developed the ability to keep the fertilized eggs inside their bodies until after the young have hatched.

Which bird never touches the ground?

Many swifts pass their whole lives without touching the ground. They are expert fliers, and because their bodies are so well adapted for flight they are not able to run or hop on the ground. Occasionally swifts fall to the ground by accident, and then they find it difficult to take off again.

Chameleons can change colour in an instant to blend with their background.

Which animals have fur?

Mammals are the main group of animals to have fur, although some mammals, such as whales, have lost theirs during the course of evolution. A few other animals have fur-like coats as well, which serve the same purpose as in mammals, to keep their body heat in. Large flying insects, such as bumblebees and hawkmoths, are often furry. These are 'cold-blooded' animals, but they have to be able to warm up their muscles before they can fly. They do this by shivering the muscles for a while. This generates heat, and the fur keeps the body warm.

Which animals, apart from birds, have feathers?

Plume Moths have wings that look as if they are made of tiny feathers. Most species of Plume Moth have five 'feathers' on each side of the body: two have evolved to replace the front wing and three have replaced the hind wing.

Do birds feed their young on milk?

Yes, a few species of bird feed their young on a rich, nutritious liquid that is similar to the milk of mammals. The birds with this unusual way of rearing their chicks are the pigeons, the Greater Flamingo and the Emperor Penguin. The milk is produced by part of the digestive system, known as the crop.

Why don't elephants have fur?

Elephants are so big that they have no need for fur. Other mammals have fur to keep in their body heat. The amount of heat a body produces is greater the higher its volume. Heat is lost through the skin, so the more skin there is, the more heat is lost. An elephant has more skin than most other animals, but what matters is the ratio between the volume of the body and the area of skin. The larger the animal, the less skin area it has in relation to its total volume. So a large animal loses much less heat than a small animal.

What is a parasite?

A parasite is an animal that lives by feeding off another organism (the host). Fleas live by sucking the blood of a larger animal and tapeworms live in the gut of larger animals and absorb food there. Some microscopic parasites absorb their food from within the blood or cells of another animal. Parasites are entirely dependent on their host for food but do not usually kill it.

Do all animals go to sleep at night?

No, some animals stay hidden and sleep during the day, and only come out at night and are described as *nocturnal*. Animals like ourselves, that are awake and active in the daytime, are called *diurnal*. There are also some animals, such as deer, that are usually active during the evening and early morning, when there is only a little light. They are said to be *crepuscular*.

How can we tell whether animals dream?

Humans experience several different types of sleep, and one is called REM (Rapid Eye Movement) sleep which is when dreams happen. Many different mammals, and some birds, show REM sleep, so it seems likely that they dream. In the case of dogs, cats, horses and chimpanzees, there is even stronger evidence. They sometimes twitch their paws or whiskers during REM sleep, and they may make noises as well, just as if they were dreaming.

Elephants do not need fur; their great bulk keeps them warm.

Which animal spends most time asleep?

The Virginia Opossum, which sleeps for 18 hours out of 24, is probably the doziest animal. But when animals hibernate, they may 'sleep' for weeks on end. Hibernation is not quite the same thing as ordinary sleep, because the animal's body temperature drops and most of its body processes slow down almost to a standstill.

Could one side of your brain go to sleep, while the other stays awake?

No, but if you were a Bottlenose Dolphin it could. Dolphins are mammals, and so have to breathe air. If they cannot get to the surface to breathe, they drown. So a dolphin cannot really afford to sleep. Its solution is to let one half of its brain sleep for an hour, then the other half. How do we know it does this? By looking at the electrical activity of the brain. The brain gives out waves of electrical activity all the time, but the sleeping brain waves look different from waking ones. Experiments show that only half the brain sleeps.

Do all animals have blood?

No – some of the simplest animals, such as sponges, sea anemones and flatworms, manage without blood. In larger, more complex and active animals, blood carries food and oxygen around the body. Very small animals, or slow-moving, simple ones, do not need to have oxygen and food moving around their bodies at high speed. These things will move about without any help, by a process known as *diffusion*. Although diffusion works slowly, it is fast enough for simple animals.

Is blood always red?

No, several different kinds of invertebrate have blue-coloured blood, and in some worms the blood is green.

What is the noisiest animal?

The loudest noise of all is made by the Blue Whale which keeps in touch with its companions using low-frequency sounds of deafening volume. They sometimes register over 180 decibels, louder than a jet engine would sound if you were standing on the runway when it took off! These sounds have been recorded over 800 kilometres away by sensitive instruments. The loudest animal in proportion to its size is the male cicada, an insect which makes a persistent buzzing sound in the breeding season. A group of cicadas in one tree registered 100 decibels, equivalent to the noise of a rock band performing.

Which animals sing?

Birds are the main songsters, of course, but some whales also produce songs, particularly the Humpback Whale. Whales sing to keep in contact with each other and to find a mate in the breeding season. Grasshoppers are also said to sing, although the sounds they make are less melodic. There is no real difference between a song and a call (such as the croak of a frog, the bark of a dog, or the squawk of a parrot). We call it a song if it is musical to human ears, but animals themselves probably do not distinguish between musical and unmusical sounds.

How many different kinds of animals use echolocation or 'radar'?

Long-eared Bat

At least three, and probably many more. The main ones are bats and *cetaceans* (whales and dolphins). Both use very high-pitched sounds (which we cannot hear) for echolocation and can detect the echoes of those sounds with astonishing accuracy. Echolocation allows bats to fly in complete darkness, and they can even 'see' thin wires stretched across their flightpath, or catch tiny flying insects that are zig-zagging through the air. Another group of animals, recently found to use echolocation, is the shrews and other small nocturnal mammals. They are not as skilled as bats or dolphins, but echolocation helps them to find their way at night.

Which animal has the most legs?

To date, this is an African Millipede which is reported to have over 700 legs. The name 'millipede' means 'thousand legs' but none actually has this many.

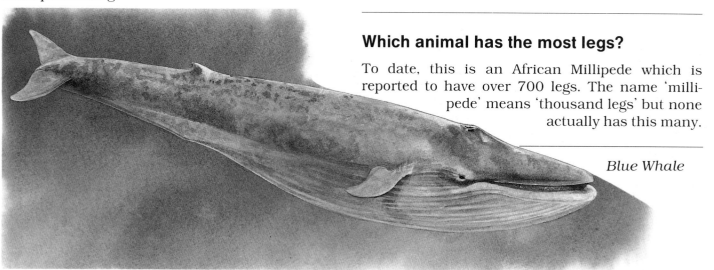

Blue Whale

Why do bats hang upside down?

Because their hindlegs are too small and weak to support them perching upright. Flying animals have to be as light as possible in order to fly. Birds have a light-weight beak instead of teeth, but bats have kept their weight down in other ways, including having tiny hindlegs. Bats are nocturnal and roost in caves or hollow trees during the day. They have little to fear from predators in their roosts, as deep caves are dark and predators tend to keep away from them. So bats can afford to have tiny hindlegs which make them slow and clumsy on the ground.

What is the longest animal in the world?

The longest animal is probably the Bootlace Worm which can be found around the coasts of Britain. One giant specimen was estimated to be at least 55 metres long. The contest for second place is between the Blue Whale, which can grow to almost 34 metres and the Whale Tapeworm, which can reach about 30 metres.

What is an arthropod?

The name *arthropod* literally means 'joint-legged'. An arthropod is an invertebrate whose body is protected by a hard outer skeleton (exoskeleton) and whose legs are jointed and occur in pairs. Examples of arthropods include insects, crabs, spiders, scorpions and centipedes. They are so successful that they occur just about everywhere on Earth: on land, in the sea, and in the air, and account for over one and a half million species.

From what sort of animal did the first mammals evolve?

The first mammals evolved from a group of meat-eating reptiles known as the *therapsids* or 'mammal-like reptiles'. These reptiles lived from about 280 to 190 million years ago and roamed the land long before the dinosaurs first appeared. Dimetrodon is perhaps the best-known example of these early reptiles. It grew to over three metres in length and was characterized by a huge crest or 'sail' arising from its back. Scientists think that this sail helped to warm the animal up more quickly in the early morning sun.

Spiders produce 'silk' to make their webs.

How many different kinds of animals produce silk?

At least three different groups. Best known are the spiders, which use silk to make webs and funnels for catching prey. One group of insects also produces silk – the moths whose caterpillars are known as silkworms. They wrap themselves up in silk before they go into the resting stage, or pupa, from which they emerge as adult moths. It is from these pupae that the thread for making silk cloth comes. The third group of animals which can produce silk are the tiny *symphylans*, related to millipedes and centipedes.

What are animals made of?

Mostly water – an animal's body is about 70–80 per cent water. The second most important ingredient is protein. Animals contain many thousands of different proteins, each with a different job to do. Some make up the muscles, tendons, and bones, others are found in blood, skin, fur and claws. Proteins form the basic fabric of every other part of the body as well. The third important ingredient is fat, used for storing energy. Fats also make up the membranes that surround each cell in the body. A fourth ingredient is only found in small amounts, but has a very important role to play. This is DNA which carries all the information needed to build up the animal's body and keep it running smoothly. Called genes, these pieces of information control almost all animal functions, and are important in reproduction, too.

SOFT-BODIED ANIMALS

Single-Celled Animals

What is a protozoan?

A protozoan is the simplest kind of animal you can find – it is made up of just one cell. One drop of pond water, when viewed through a microscope, can contain hundreds of these tiny creatures. More than 50,000 different kinds of protozoans are known to exist.

How do single-celled animals move about?

Single-celled animals get about in three different ways. Some have a tiny whip-like structure (a *flagellum*) protruding from them. They wave this to push themselves along; others may be surrounded by tiny little hairs (*cilia*) which beat rhythmically to produce movement. Amoebas crawl along by extending a section of cell. The rest of the body then catches up and the process is repeated.

How does an amoeba reproduce itself?

To make two individuals, an amoeba simply splits itself in two. When an amoeba is fully grown, the nucleus – the 'control centre' which contains all the hereditary material – divides itself equally in two, closely followed by an equal division of the jelly-like substance (*cytoplasm*) which makes up the rest of the amoeba's body. The resulting two amoebae are identical.

What causes malaria?

The tiny protozoan *Plasmodium vivax* is the culprit. It normally lives in the salivary glands of the female *anopheles* mosquito, but will make straight for the liver of any person who happens to be bitten by the mosquito. In the liver, the *Plasmodium* multiplies and then infects red blood cells, causing them to burst. The disease is passed from person to person by the female mosquito sucking the blood of an infected person, and then passing the *Plasmodium* on to an uninfected person at her next meal.

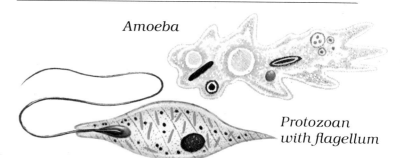

Amoeba

Protozoan with flagellum

Is a euglena a plant or an animal?

It is both. Normally, a euglena gets its energy from sunlight, like a plant, but if it is kept in the dark it is capable of absorbing food particles through its cell walls, like a simple animal.

Is a sponge an animal?

Yes, a sponge is an animal, but not in the normal way we think of one. It has no nervous system, and no muscles with which to move about. Instead it may be thought of as a collection of individual cells which have organized themselves into a single body and anchored themselves to the sea bed.

Simple Animals

What is coral made of?

Coral is made of the tiny limestone 'skeletons' of individual animals known as *coral polyps*. As each polyp matures, it sends out filaments from which another polyp grows, burying its parent beneath it. This process, known as *budding*, never ceases, so that over a period of time, large structures of coral can develop. The shape of these structures depends on the species of coral, as each has its own characteristic pattern of budding.

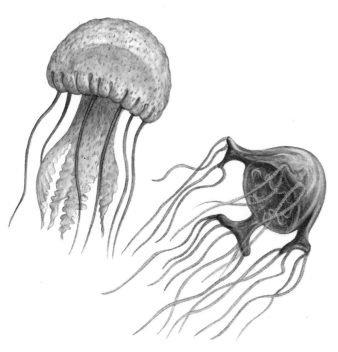

Two types of jellyfish. Their long tentacles contain powerful poisons.

How do jellyfish swim?

Jellyfish are typically bell-shaped, semi-transparent animals which swim by a method of jet propulsion. They thrust themselves through the water by alternately opening and shutting their central 'bell'. This squirts a jet of water out behind them and so pushes the jellyfish along. All jellyfish have sophisticated balancing organs which help them to keep upright in the water.

What is a Water Bear?

A type of microscopic animal, that belongs to the invertebrates, but does not fit into any known group of animals. Water Bears are so called because they have a sausage-shaped body, sturdy legs and a head with a pointed 'snout', rather like a microscopic bear or pig. Scientists think they may be related to insects, but they do not have wings and most of them are much smaller than the smallest insects. Water Bears are often found in drainpipes and gutters, or living on the surface of moss plants.

What is a hydra?

A hydra is a tiny cylindrical freshwater animal, usually anchored at one end to a piece of underwater vegetation or debris, and with an array of stinging tentacles at the other. It lives in streams and ponds and reproduces by budding. When conditions are favourable, a small bulge forms on the parent hydra. This eventually detaches itself and becomes a new individual.

How do sea anemones capture their prey?

Sometimes mistaken for plants, these sedentary animals rely on chance encounter to capture their prey. Any creature, including quite large fish, which happens to brush against the waving tentacles of a sea anemone is at once immobilized by its powerful stinging cells and then dragged into the anemone's bag-like stomach.

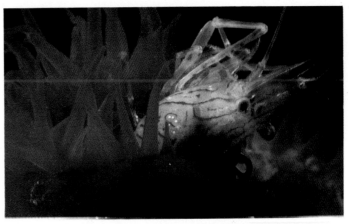

An anemone uses its stinging tentacles to paralyse its prey.

11

How does a Portuguese Man o' War differ from a true jellyfish?

The Portuguese Man o' War is a *colonial* jellyfish. Each Man o' War is made up of thousands of individual animals which collectively behave as one organism. Each individual in the colony has its own job to do: some are concerned with feeding, some with swimming, others with reproduction. The Portuguese Man o' War is a fearsome-looking creature. It has extremely long trailing tentacles armed with poisonous stings, which paralyse any fish that comes into contact with it.

Portuguese Man O'War

What creature eats jellyfish stings?

Sea Slugs eat jellyfish stings. The Sea Slug takes in the stinging cells of its prey, the jellyfish, and conveys them to the tentacles on its back. There the stinging cells give the same protection to the Sea Slug as they did to their original owner.

Sea Slug

Is all coral hard?

No, some corals are soft and flexible with very little limestone in their bodies. Many grow into elaborate shapes which sway on the sea bed like exotic plants.

Coral reef

Where do coral reefs occur?

Certain conditions have to be just right for coral to thrive. The coral polyp is closely associated with tiny plants called algae, so coral will only grow in waters that are both light enough and warm enough for algae to *photosynthesize* (make sugar using sunlight). This usually means in water which is clear, no deeper than 50 metres (or sunlight will not penetrate sufficiently) and above 20°C.

Can you eat a Sea Gooseberry?

A Sea Gooseberry is a sea animal rather like a jellyfish – and not very palatable, unless you happen to be a jellyfish. Its transparent, gooseberry-shaped body bears a pair of long trailing tentacles which it uses to catch and immobilize small animals.

How do jellyfish reproduce?

Jellyfish reproduce by shedding sperm and eggs into the sea. The fertilized egg then settles on the sea bed and grows into a creature rather like a sea anemone called a polyp. This polyp sometimes sprouts other polyps, but finally it sprouts in a different way to produce miniature jellyfish, which wriggle away.

Worms and Flukes

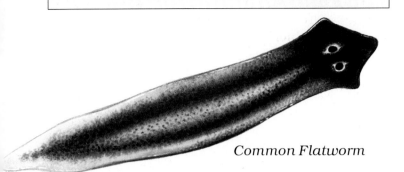

Common Flatworm

What is the difference between a flatworm and a fluke?

At first glance, flatworms and flukes seem quite similar – small, flat, soft-bodied creatures which live in water or damp surroundings. Flatworms tend to live on the sea bed or at the bottom of ponds and streams and are free-swimming, while flukes are parasitic and spend a good part of their lives hidden in the bodies of other animals (often fish and mammals)..

Why is it important to cook pork very thoroughly?

The Pork Tapeworm, a parasite of the digestive system, causes wasting disease in humans by absorbing food from the human intestine. Its eggs are passed out with human faeces, and, if allowed to contaminate pig food, will hatch out in the pig's intestine and migrate to the pig's muscle tissue. If pork is not thoroughly cooked before it is eaten (so killing the tapeworm), that tapeworm can then re-infect someone else.

Is it true that if you cut an earthworm in half, you will have two earthworms?

No. Only the front half will grow a new tail. The rear half cannot grow a new head. Other simpler animals can regenerate both ends but this amazing facility is lost as the animals become more complex.

Common Earthworm

How long can a tapeworm grow?

A Pork Tapeworm can grow to over four metres, while a Whale Tapeworm can reach up to 30 metres! Bathed in nutrient solution, a tapeworm has no need for a complex digestive system. Its simple body consists of a succession of identical reproductive segments linked to a sucker-like head which attaches itself to its host's gut wall.

Which blood fluke infects millions of people around the world?

Schistosoma is a blood fluke which is common in Africa and southern Asia. Rice paddies are favourite breeding grounds for this water-dwelling fluke, which spends part of its life cycle inside freshwater snails. The larvae which break out of the snail burrow into the skin of any available human, invading the blood vessels of the intestine and causing swelling and bleeding.

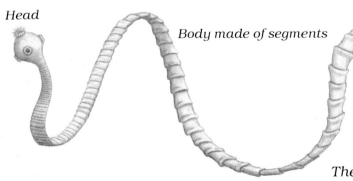

Head

Body made of segments

The Pork Tapeworm can grow to 10 metres in the human intestine.

How many eggs can a Fish Tapeworm produce during its lifetime?

It is possible that a ten-year-old Fish Tapeworm may have produced as many as two thousand million eggs. As each segment of the tapeworm ripens, it becomes a 'bag of eggs' which then breaks off and passes out of the fish's intestine. Because of the complexity of the tapeworm's life cycle, it has to produce large numbers of eggs to ensure that at least a few survive to adulthood.

How can you tell a female earthworm from a male earthworm?

You can't. Earthworms are both male and female at the same time. When a pair of earthworms mate, they exchange sperm and store them in special organs called *spermathecas*. Later the sperm will fertilize the eggs in a cocoon made by the clitellum or saddle.

The Medicinal Leech was used to 'suck out poisons' from the body.

How big is a Giant Earthworm?

Compared to a Common Earthworm, it is enormous! The biggest earthworm in the world, the South African Giant Earthworm, may grow as long as seven metres and have a body two or three centimetres thick.

How were leeches used by doctors?

Leeches are a type of worm which suck the blood of animals by attaching themselves with suckers and using tiny, jagged-edged teeth to pierce the skin. Because they can take as much as ten times their weight in blood in a single meal, they were once used by 19th-century doctors for drawing 'bad blood' from their unfortunate patients.

What is a tubifex?

A thin, red worm that lives in thick mud on the bottom of rivers and streams. If you keep aquarium fish, then you are probably already familiar with them, as they are commonly sold as live fish food.

Giant Earthworm

Animals with Shells

What is a mollusc?

A mollusc is an animal whose soft, unsegmented body is covered by a tissue called a *mantle*. The mantle often secretes a shell, which may lie outside the body, as in limpets, or inside, as in cuttlefish. Some molluscs (such as the octopus) may not even have a shell.

Why is a Cowrie shell so glossy and patterned on the outside?

The shells of all molluscs are secreted by their *mantles* – the protective fold of skin covering their soft bodies. Because the Cowrie is able to extend its mantle right over its shell like a cloak, it is able to lay down shell from both sides, making the outside as glossy and as beautiful as the inside.

What is a bivalve?

A bivalve is a mollusc whose shell is divided into two halves. The two halves are joined together by a muscular hinge, along which the bulk of the animal's body lies. Bivalves tend to be filter feeders with limited powers of movement. Some bivalves, notably the scallops, have developed methods of 'swimming' to escape from predators. They expel a water jet as they snap their two shells shut and this propels them through the water.

How does the Tropical Cone Shell kill its prey?

The Cone Shell is a single-shelled mollusc that has adapted its tongue in an ingenious way for capturing prey. On its tongue are long teeth, which bear a poison so lethal that is can kill a human being. When a suitable prey comes within striking distance, the Cone Shell uses its tongue as a gun to fire poisoned darts into it. The paralysed victim is then dragged back to the shell and slowly devoured.

How do the eggs of a Garden Snail differ from those of a slug?

Snail eggs have a calcium-containing shell, and therefore are protected to some extent from water-logging or drying out. Slug eggs, however, do not have such a shell and so need to be laid in a very damp place (such as underneath a rotting log) if they are to hatch out.

What do chiton shells look like?

Chiton shells are unusual in that they consist of a series of eight separate plates rather than one single shell. Sometimes referred to as 'coat-of-mail shells', these small, flattened creatures are found on rocky shores clinging to rocks or any other hard surface. If they become detached from the rock, they tend to curl up in a ball to protect their soft bodies.

How does the shell of a nautilus help it to swim?

By providing a buoyancy aid. The shell of a nautilus is mainly filled with air pockets, and the actual body of the nautilus is for the most part situated outside the shell. As the nautilus grows, another air pocket is created in the shell, to compensate for the extra weight of flesh.

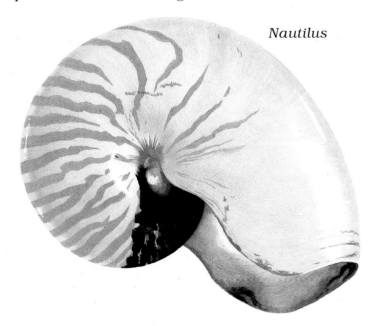

Nautilus

Octopuses and Squids

What is the difference between an octopus and a squid?

An octopus is an eight-armed mollusc which has given up its shell. A squid has ten arms (two of which are longer than the others) and a reduced internal shell, known as the *pen skeleton*. The body of a squid is also more cylindrical and tapering; the octopus's is more sac-like. Both have extremely good eyesight, and both use jet propulsion to swim through the water, although the squid tends to be the better swimmer.

How big is a Giant Squid?

Squids are capable of growing to enormous sizes. Some grow as long as 15 metres or more and have eyes greater than 30 centimetres across. Sperm Whales prey on squid, and frequently appear with large scars on their snouts, suggesting that they have been battling with squids of even larger proportions than any which have been caught.

How does the Australian Blue-ringed Octopus protect her eggs?

The Australian Blue-ringed Octopus is one of the few animals which manages to pass the poison in its bite on to its eggs. So even if a potential predator succeeds in avoiding the mother's lethal injection, it will succumb to the toxin stored within the eggs. The developing young octopuses inherit their parents' natural immunity to their own poisons.

What is special about the eyes of a squid?

The eyes of a squid, apart from being very large, are very complex and, in many ways, better than human eyes. Squids can see in much finer detail than we can, but focus on objects in an entirely different way. They alter the distance between the lens and the retina, rather than changing the shape of the lens as we do. Squids tend to have very large brains to cope with this visual information, and very quick reflexes.

How does an octopus capture its prey?

The octopus puts its eight long arms to very good use when hunting prey. It pounces on its prey (usually crabs and lobsters) and then uses its tentacles to clasp the victim to its horny mouth in a deathly embrace.

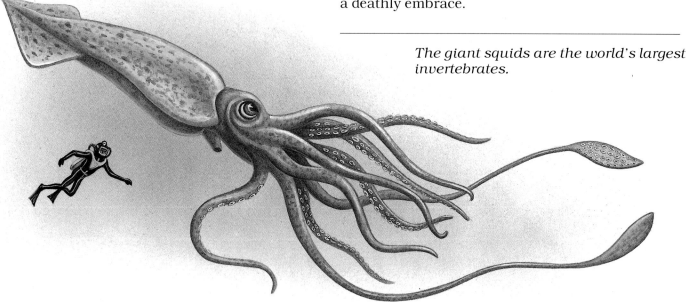

The giant squids are the world's largest invertebrates.

Echinoderms

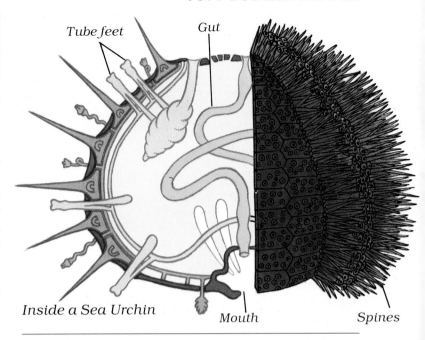

Tube feet   Gut

Inside a Sea Urchin   Mouth   Spines

What are echinoderms?

The echinoderms are a group of spiny-skinned animals, which include such creatures as starfish, sea urchins, brittlestars and featherstars. They are usually symmetrical and have their organs arranged in multiples of five. For example, starfish normally have five arms, but some may have as many as 50.

Is a Sea Cucumber a plant?

The soft cylindrical bodies of Sea Cucumbers are often mistaken for exotic sea plants but in fact they are animals related to starfish, and move on their sides along the sea bed. Their mouths, located at one end of the body, are surrounded by a ring of tentacles, which are used for feeding on decaying matter and plankton.

Can a starfish, if turned upside down, right itself?

A starfish on its back is capable of righting itself by twisting one of its arms over to grip a hard surface. Once the starfish has established a firm foothold, it folds itself in half and slowly somersaults back into its more normal position.

Starfish, Sea Cucumber and Sea Urchin

How does a Sea Urchin walk along the sea bottom?

A Sea Urchin moves with the help of its spines, and its tube feet, which are arranged in five columns up and down its body. The tube feet end in minute suction pads, which are able to grip any firm surface with which the Sea Urchin comes into contact. By extending and retracting these tiny suckers, the Sea Urchin is able to move quite rapidly over difficult terrain.

How does a Sea Cucumber defend itself?

The Sea Cucumber has a most extraordinary way of defending itself. If startled or threatened, it will simply pass all its internal organs out through its anus, creating a sticky mass of tangled tubes which often ensnares its would-be predator. The Sea Cucumber then crawls away on its tube feet (which run down its sides), and regenerates its entrails within two or three weeks.

How brittle is a brittle-star?

Brittle-stars are commonly found washed up on the seashore, and you can easily recognize them by their five long wavy arms attached to a small, central disc-like body. But handle them with care! Their arms will snap under the slightest pressure.

INSECTS

What is an insect?

Insects are often thought of as small creatures which fly, buzz or scuttle around on a variable number of legs. This description is not quite accurate enough. All insects – whether they are butterflies, moths, ants, flies, grasshoppers or silverfish – have certain features in common. Every insect has three pairs of legs and the body is divided into three parts: head, thorax and abdomen. On its head is a single pair of antennae or feelers, a pair of *compound* eyes, usually three small *simple* eyes, and a set of mouthparts which work sideways rather than up and down. Most, though not all, insects also have wings.

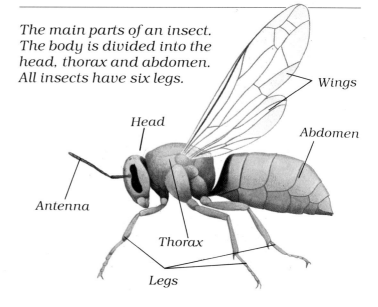

The main parts of an insect. The body is divided into the head, thorax and abdomen. All insects have six legs.

Head

Wings

Abdomen

Antenna

Thorax

Legs

How does an insect breathe?

Insects breathe through a system of tubes which open to the air through tiny holes (called *spiracles*) on the abdomen and thorax. Inside the insect's body the tubes, called *tracheae*, branch repeatedly and end in the muscles. Normally oxygen passes through the tracheae into the tissue, and carbon dioxide passes out. Larger insects, such as bees and wasps, have air sacs in the muscles which can take in extra air as the muscles expand and contract. This increases the supply of oxygen to the muscles.

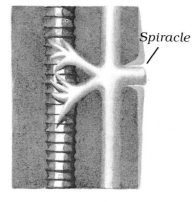

Muscle

Spiracle

Insects do not have lungs. Air passes directly into the muscles.

How does an insect see through a compound eye?

An insect's eye is not one single organ like that of a mammal but is a collection of many tiny separate 'eyes'. The images from all the lenses combine to give a mosaic picture of the world. While this picture is nothing like the detailed image humans can see, it does enable the insect to detect the slightest movement. Insects such as dragonflies have eyes covering most of their heads and can detect predators coming at them from all angles. Flies are difficult to swat for the same reason.

How many insects are there in the world?

Nobody really knows, but some estimates have put the number at around one thousand million thousand million. In other words, for every human being alive in the world, there are about 200 million insects.

Can insects see in colour?

Honeybees and butterflies certainly can, and they use this ability to recognize flowers. Honeybees cannot see red, but this is more than compensated for by their ability to distinguish ultraviolet 'colour', which is invisible to humans. Butterflies also use their colour vision to recognize potential mates during courtship.

What is the function of an insect's simple eyes?

No one seems to know quite what the three simple eyes on an insect's head are supposed to do. In some insects, such as moths and bees, they are practically obscured by scales or hairs, while in others, such as beetles, they are completely absent. All dragonflies possess them, but it is difficult to know what function they perform when the dragonflies already possess such marvellously efficient compound eyes. It has been suggested that the simple eyes may act as stimulators to the compound eyes, quickening the responses of the insect to changes in brightness of light.

What is metamorphosis?

Metamorphosis is the name given to the changes that insects go through as they grow from the egg to the adult. There are two types: insects such as grasshoppers pass through three stages, each resembling the adult more closely. This is incomplete metamorphosis. Complete metamorphosis, as in the butterfly, involves four stages: egg, larva, pupa and adult. The intermediate stages bear no resemblance to the adult.

The Four stages of metamorphosis: egg 1. larva 2. pupa 3. and adult 4.

What is an exoskeleton?

The exoskeleton is the tough outer casing which surrounds an insect's body, protecting its soft internal organs. Unlike animals such as birds and mammals, an insect has no internal skeleton, and relies on the exoskeleton for rigidity and muscular support.

What are the main drawbacks of an exoskeleton?

Because the exoskeleton is so stiff it does not expand easily. As the insect grows in size it has to moult or shed its outer casing and then grow another. During this moulting period the insect is vulnerable to attack from predators. Another drawback is that the bigger the insect becomes, the heavier its exoskeleton, and the more difficult it becomes to move and fly. This is why insects tend to be small.

Do all insects undergo metamorphosis?

No – insects such as bristletails, silverfish and springtails develop without metamorphosis. The young insect is virtually the same as the adult, except that it is smaller, often with fewer segments, and is unable to reproduce. As it increases its size, it sheds its skin and replaces it with a new skin big enough to fit the larger body.

Can insects reproduce without mating?

A variety of insect groups can reproduce without mating. The best known are the aphids (the group which includes the greenfly). During the summer the adult females produce up to 25 new females a day from unfertilized eggs. Quite why this process, called *parthenogenesis*, occurs is not well understood.

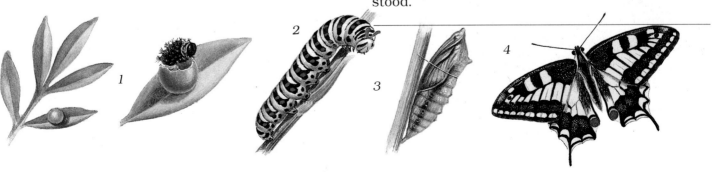

Springtails and Bristletails

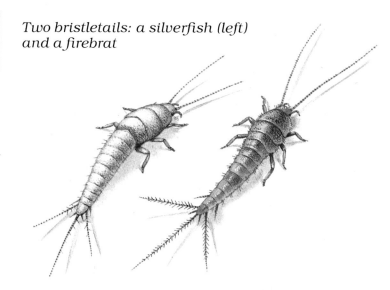

Two bristletails: a silverfish (left) and a firebrat

What are springtails and bristletails?

Springtails and bristletails are small wingless insects which exist in enormous numbers all over the world. Springtails are usually inconspicuous, soil-dwelling creatures, with spring-like tails which enable them to leap forwards by several centimetres at a time. Bristletails, on the other hand, have smooth, tapering bodies, long antennae and long, slender tail feelers, and tend to live on rotting vegetation.

Which is the most numerous insect group in the world?

Springtails are the most numerous of all animals in the world: indeed, it has been estimated that there may be as many as 250 million springtails in just one acre of meadowland. They have also colonized every corner of the Earth's land surface, from the frozen wastes of Antarctica to the highest mountain top.

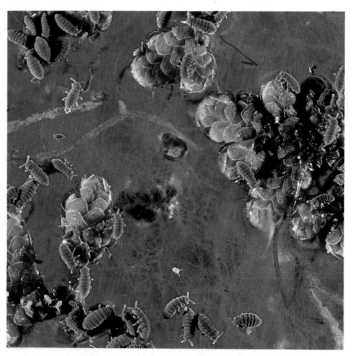

Springtails: the most common insects in the world

Which small, silvery insect can frequently be seen scuttling about in kitchen cupboards?

The distinctive silverfish, a member of the bristletail group, has a glistening tapering body covered in scales that easily rub off. It is probably the most familiar insect in damp kitchens and bathrooms. It leads a secretive, nocturnal life and dislikes bright light – hence its hurried movements to hide when the cupboard is suddenly opened.

How do silverfish reproduce?

Silverfish are unusual in becoming sexually mature before they are fully grown. Whereas other more advanced insects are not ready to mate until they have completed their last moult, silverfish continue to moult and reproduce throughout their surprisingly long lives of several years. During the courtship ritual, the male performs a dance and then deposits a tiny packet of sperm on the ground. The female picks it up with her lower abdomen, where the eggs are fertilized.

Which insect actively seeks out warm, domestic environments?

The firebrat prefers warm, even hot, places and can sometimes be found swarming in bakeries at temperatures that would normally discourage other insects. Its liking for warmth is evidence of its origins in hot, dry lands.

Dragonflies

What is the difference between a dragonfly and a damselfly?

Dragonflies and damselflies are both brilliantly coloured fresh-water-loving insects. Whereas dragonflies spread their wings away from the body when at rest, damselflies hold their wings erect over their backs, as do butterflies. The damselfly tends to be smaller, with a more slender body, and its flight is usually weak and fluttering, while dragonflies are noted for their powerful and direct flight.

Damselfly

Which insect lives only for a day in its adult form?

The mayfly, with its soft body and feeble flight, lives for only a few hours in its adult form, during which time its sole purpose is to mate and lay eggs. The insect may take as long as three years to complete its life cycle and to become an adult.

What stage in the mayfly's life sets it apart from all other insects?

The winged insect that emerges when the mayfly nymph crawls out of the water, is not the true adult. This stage is known as the subimago, and the mayfly has to shed its skin yet again before the glistening body of the true adult or imago appears. Mayflies are the only insects known to undergo this subimaginal stage.

How does a dragonfly use its legs in flight?

The long spiny legs of a dragonfly are usually laid against the body during flight, offering minimal resistance to the air. As soon as the dragonfly spots a potential prey, it holds its legs forward to form a basket, open at the front, in which the victim is caught.

How does the dragonfly nymph capture its prey?

The dragonfly nymph is a ferocious predator which lives at the bottom of ponds. It captures its prey by means of a mask – a feature unique to dragonflies and damselflies. The mask is made up of a greatly enlarged bottom lip equipped with a pair of sharp claws, and shoots out at the sight of any small and moving animal. At rest, the mask is folded underneath the head.

Dragonfly nymph

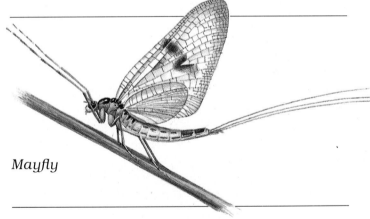
Mayfly

Why are some damselflies considered to be 'ghostly spirits'?

In tropical America the largest damselflies are bigger than the largest dragonflies and have bodies measuring 12 centimetres in length with wing-spans of 17 centimetres. At dusk when they fly, only the coloured tips of their transparent wings can be seen. This gives a rather ghostly effect which some native peoples consider to be 'spirits of the dead'.

Stick and Leaf Insects

Which is the longest insect in the world?

The Giant Stick Insect of Indonesia, which can grow up to 32 centimetres long, must rank as the longest insect alive.

Why are stick and leaf insects so-called?

It is not hard to see why stick and leaf insects are named as they are. Practically indistinguishable from a background of twigs, leaves and branches, the stick and leaf insects are camouflage experts. They rest motionless during the day, their long twig-like bodies blending perfectly with the surrounding branches, and move and feed only at night. Even their eggs are camouflaged to look like the seeds of the plant on which they live. These curious insects occur mainly in the tropical regions of Asia.

How do some stick insects change colour?

Stick insects are usually coloured in shades of green or brown. The pure green individuals are unable to change colour, but the brown forms change frequently, becoming paler by day and darker by night. This is caused by the movement of brown pigment granules within their skin cells. The brown pigments move to the surface and spread out at dusk, making the insect appear darker. By day the pigments move to the inner part of the cell and form clumps, giving the insect a pale appearance.

A stick insect (above) and leaf insect (below)

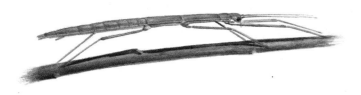

Stick insects are perfectly camouflaged against trees and branches.

Why is nearly every stick insect female?

Stick insects reproduce without needing to mate, like aphids. The egg is not fertilized and consequently in many species of stick insect the male is either unknown or redundant. The female lays the eggs singly, simply dropping them on to the forest floor, and in certain forests of North America, the sound of thousands of eggs dropping from the Common Walking Stick Insect is as loud as falling rain.

Why do stick insects make good pets?

Stick insects are probably the most commonly kept pet insects. They are slow-moving, easy to breed and can often be fed on leaves of ivy, privet or lilac. However, it is important that the insects are kept at a constantly warm temperature, because they cannot survive the cold winters of northern Europe.

Cockroaches and Mantids

What do cockroaches and Praying Mantids have in common?

German cockroach

Praying Mantid

The wings of both types of insect bear such similarities that scientists have placed them in the same order (*Dictyoptera*). Both types of insect have thick leathery forewings and broad delicate hindwings. Only the forewings are used in flight, the hindwings are folded like a fan underneath the protective forewings. Both types of insect lay their eggs in little cases which are like miniature handbags.

Why are cockroaches regarded as pests?

With their furtive, nocturnal lifestyle and scavenging habits, the sight of a cockroach scurrying across the kitchen floor is a most unwelcome one. Fouling more food with their droppings than they actually eat, cockroaches emit an unpleasant smell. If they live somewhere dirty they can carry germs. They hide during the day in warm places where their numbers can increase rapidly.

Why are cockroaches sometimes referred to as 'ancient insects'?

To describe cockroaches as ancient insects is in fact a tribute to their evolutionary design: they are not particularly specialized, they will eat practically anything, and can squeeze themselves out of harm's way into the smallest crevices. Fossils of cockroaches, very like the modern forms, have been found dating back 300 million years, and the fact that they were so diverse and widespread then suggests that they must have been in existence for at least 400 million years.

Do cockroaches make good mothers?

Cockroaches are extremely caring towards their eggs. Many carry their eggs about with them in little capsules for weeks until they are ready to hatch, others glue them into a crevice where they are difficult to detect. This 'caring' trait has obviously contributed to the insect's evolutionary success.

A Praying Mantid devours its prey.

Do Praying Mantids really pray?

Praying Mantids hold their spiny forelegs together, raised in an attitude of worship, which is why they are called praying, though their fierce habits should warrant the name preying instead. Praying Mantids are fierce and efficient hunters, and will only eat other insects that they have captured alive. They are usually very well camouflaged and hunt their victims by lying in wait.

23

Butterflies and Moths

Bee Hawkmoth

Convolvulous Hawkmoth

Peacock

Red Admiral

What is the difference between a butterfly and a moth?

People tend to think of moths as dull-coloured, night-flying insects with fat, furry bodies, and butterflies as brightly coloured, day-flying insects. In fact there are many brightly coloured moths which fly by day. The Six-spot Burnet Moth and the Emperor Moth are two examples. To a scientist, the real difference lies in the shape of their antennae and the linkage between the fore- and hindwings. A butterfly's antennae are long and slender, and tipped with knobs, while the moth's antennae are thin and feathery. At rest, most butterflies fold their wings over their bodies, revealing their underside pattern, while moths hold their wings either spread out flat or at separate angles to each other.

Why are the wings of butterflies and moths dusty to touch?

Butterflies and moths belong to the order *Lepidoptera* which means 'scaly wings'. If you happen to touch a butterfly's or moth's wings, your fingers will become covered with a fine dust. This fine dust is made of the minute, overlapping scales that cover the insect's wings and which produce the intricate and often brilliant markings for which butterflies (and some moths) are noted.

How do butterflies defend themselves against predators?

Butterflies are not as delicate and defenceless as they may at first seem. The Monarch Butterfly is extremely tough and foul-tasting to birds, and can even manage to withstand the occasional peck. False wing markings on wing tails may fool predators into biting sections of the wings which are expendable, and the undersides of a butterfly's wings may provide superb camouflage against surrounding vegetation. Large, bright eye-spot markings, like those on the Peacock Butterfly, may also serve to startle a potential foe.

How do the scales on a butterfly's wings produce such vivid patterns?

Each scale on a butterfly's wing is coloured, and interlocks with the other scales on the wing to form a pattern rather like a mosaic picture. The white and red colours are produced by pigments in the scales, while the blues and metallic hues are caused by the way certain wavelengths of light are reflected off the structural surface of the scales.

Why do male Purple Emperor Butterflies like to drink from rotting animal corpses?

The male Purple Emperor Butterfly may occasionally be spotted feeding from dung or rotten animal corpses on the woodland floor in order to increase the supply of sodium salts to his reproductive organs. These extra salts are then passed on to the female for use in egg production.

Where do butterflies go in winter?

Most butterflies of temperate regions such as North America and northern Europe spend the winter as eggs or pupae. Some, such as the Red Admiral, hibernate in the adult form. Others migrate southwards to warmer areas.

Where will you find butterfly trees?

There is a type of conifer that grows in Mexico, California and Florida that provides a home, year after year, for millions of Monarch Butterflies during the winter. Here the butterflies cling to the trees in such dense clusters that the trees appear to be dripping with butterflies. The butterflies rest here until the spring, when the warmer weather dictates that they should migrate northwards.

Which butterfly depends on ants to complete its life cycle?

The Large Blue Butterfly has a remarkable life cycle, part of which is spent in the company of an ant (the *Myrmica* ant). The adult butterfly lays her eggs on the thyme plant, on which the caterpillar feeds during the first few weeks of life. The caterpillar leaves the plant and is 'discovered' by ants, which are attracted to the sweet substance given off by the caterpillar. The caterpillar is carried off by the ants to their nest, where they milk the caterpillar, which in turn feeds on the young ant larvae. The caterpillar spends the winter in the nest, pupates, and finally emerges from the nest as an adult.

How does the caterpillar of the Elephant Hawk Moth defend itself?

The caterpillar of the Elephant Hawk Moth is about seven centimetres long, brown, and with four large eye-spots near its head. If disturbed by a toad, it draws in its head and the body segments behind the head bulge out, making the eye-spots seem huge. This makes the caterpillar look like a miniature snake to the toad, which adopts a defensive posture, blowing up its body and rising up on its legs.

How do moths protect themselves from bats?

Bats hunt by a sophisticated method of echo-location. They send out high-pitched sound waves and use the echoes to judge the position of potential prey. Some American moths have developed the ability to tune in to the bat's sonar system; as soon as they detect a bat approaching, they fall to the ground like a stone. Others dive into a spiral, while others manage to block the bat's signal or send back confusing high-pitched sounds.

Ants take the caterpillars of the Large Blue Butterfly to their nest and there extract food from them.

Why are moths attracted to bright light at night?

The allure of a bright light source is perhaps best explained by the moth's reaction to fixed natural light, such as the moon. When the distant light of the moon is received by one section of the compound eye, the moth tries to keep that part of the eye illuminated, and it flies in a straight line until otherwise diverted. If the light is relatively near, then the moth will fly in a curve. This curved flight pattern develops into a spiral as the moth descends on to the light source.

Grasshoppers

How does the grasshopper sing?

A grasshopper produces its familiar chirping sound by rubbing its hindlegs over the ribs of its forewings. On the inner side of the femur, or 'thigh' of each hindleg, is a row of tiny, evenly spaced pegs, and these are stroked over the prominent veins on the forewings. Usually it is only the male who sings.

Grasshopper

Where are a grasshopper's ears?

The 'ears' of a grasshopper are found on its abdomen, and they consist of a rigid structure supporting an ear drum, rather like that in a human ear. These sound receptors respond to changes in air pressure, and this information is relayed to the brain via nerve fibres.

Do all grasshoppers sing the same song?

Rather like birds, each species of grasshopper has its own distinct song.

Which insect can tell you the temperature?

The American Tree Cricket, or 'Thermometer Cricket', is so sensitive to heat while it is singing that you can work out the temperature in degrees Fahrenheit by timing its rate of chirping. Simply count the number of chirps in 15 seconds, and add 39!

Why do locusts swarm?

A locust is a large tropical or subtropical grasshopper. Occasionally they form vast migratory swarms. There are two phases to a locust's life: a solitary, grasshopper phase, and a swarming locust phase. When scattered, solitary locusts come together to lay their eggs, their numbers build up, inducing colour changes in the immature 'hoppers' to bold black and yellow stripes. The activity of these hoppers increases by mutual stimulation, and they start to march in bands. As they develop into adults, they form enormous migrating swarms, sometimes hundreds of square kilometres in extent. When they descend to feed, they devour every green leaf in sight for miles around.

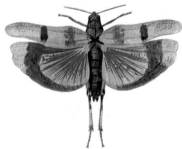

(above) Grasshopper nymph. Locust at rest (below left) and in flight (below right)

Termites

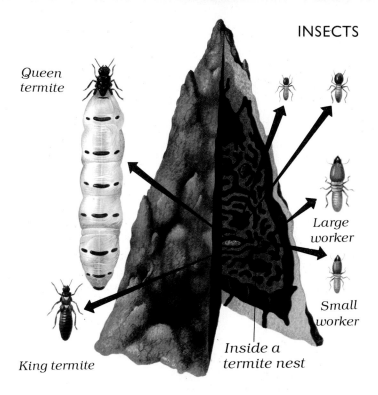

Queen termite

Large worker

Small worker

King termite

Inside a termite nest

Why are termites called White Ants?

Termites are pale, soft-bodied insects and, like ants, they live in large, underground colonies. They also have a caste system to separate the different functions of its members. But those are the only similarities. Termites have straight antennae, but an ant's antennae are bent. An ant's body has a 'waist' between the thorax and abdomen, but the termite does not. Ants and termites evolved along similar lines, but in fact, termites are more closely related to cockroaches than to ants.

What do termites eat?

Many termites feed on wood, although they cannot digest the wood by themselves. Inside the gut live tiny cellulose-digesting protozoans, which do most of the work of digestion. Without these protozoans, the termites could not survive.

How long does a termite queen live?

In the more advanced termites, the termite queen may live for 50 years or more. Accommodated within a royal chamber deep inside the termite mound, she becomes so enlarged in pregnancy that she is unable to move. The queen is a sophisticated egg-laying machine and lays an egg every two seconds.

Why are termites considered to be the greatest insect builders?

The nests of some of the tropical and subtropical termites are amazing structures. With enormous towers rising some five or six metres, these massive and internally intricate buildings provide homes for millions of sexless workers. The structures tend to be double-walled, the outer wall being made from an extremely hard cement mixed from saliva, excrement and clay. In West Africa, where it rains heavily, the colonies build mushroom-shaped nests to provide a roof against the rain. Each season, the termites build a new mushroom roof.

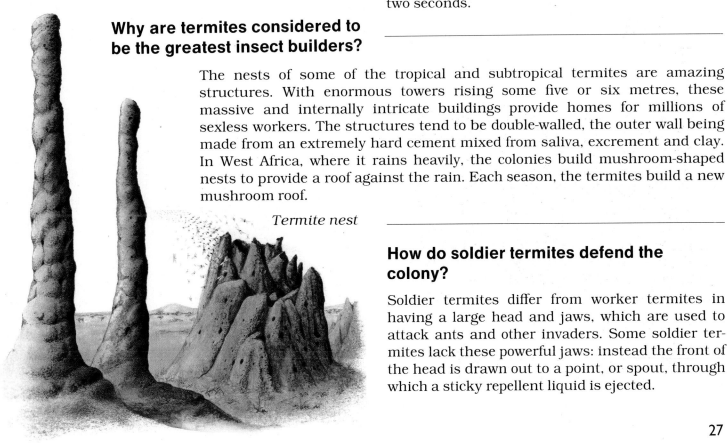

Termite nest

How do soldier termites defend the colony?

Soldier termites differ from worker termites in having a large head and jaws, which are used to attack ants and other invaders. Some soldier termites lack these powerful jaws: instead the front of the head is drawn out to a point, or spout, through which a sticky repellent liquid is ejected.

Bugs and Beetles

What is the difference between a bug and beetle?

Bugs and beetles are regarded by scientists as two different groups, even though their differences may not be obvious to the untrained eye. Both bugs and beetles exhibit an enormous variety of shapes, colours and sizes, but bugs are all united in having a set of piercing and sucking mouthparts. These are used to suck up liquid food, unlike the mouth-parts of beetles which are adapted for chewing. Beetles have modified their forewings into hard protective coverings for the hindwings, whereas in bugs the forewings are either partially leathery and protect the hindwings, or they are the same membranous texture as the hindwings.

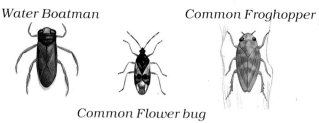

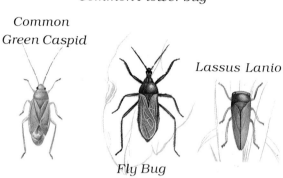

Four different kinds of bug

Are fireflies hot to touch?

Fireflies are named after the brilliant light they give out when flying, but this light is not at all hot. Emanating from the underside of the tip of the abdomen, this light has a strange coldness, due to the efficiency with which the light is produced. (An average electric light bulb will waste about 97 per cent of the energy supplied as heat, whereas a firefly will convert energy to light with less than 10 per cent waste.)

The female glow-worm uses light to attract a mate.

Is a glow-worm a worm or an insect?

A glow-worm is a insect – or a beetle to be more precise. It has the name glow-worm because the female is wingless and looks more like a worm than a beetle.

Why do glow-worms glow in the dark?

Glow-worms glow in the dark to attract mates. Both sexes give out light, although why the male does isn't clear, as he has very large eyes with which to search out females. At night the female climbs up among the grass and displays her luminous abdomen, which attracts winged males from great distances.

Which insects care for their young?

The Sexton Beetle is one of the few insects in which the male and female stay together as a couple to look after their young. The two adult beetles find a small dead animal and bury it. Once the animal is entombed, the beetles mate, and the female lays her eggs above this pool of rotting flesh. The larvae are fed by the parents with regurgitated food, and only when the grubs become pupae do the adults dig their way out and fly away.

How do pond skaters walk on water?

Pond skaters rely on the surface tension of water to support their weight. They hold their second and third pairs of legs wide apart, their tips causing dimples on the water surface. They prefer slow-moving or stagnant water, where the suface tension is not disrupted.

Do Lantern Flies give out light?

None of the Lantern Flies is luminous: the name arose because early entomologists (scientists who study insects) thought that such curiously shaped and brightly coloured insects ought to give out light.

Which insect has the loudest song?

Not only are some cicadas the noisiest of insects; they also rank among the biggest. Their singing apparatus consists of a pair of compartments at the base of the abdomen. Each has a stiff inner wall which can be pulled up and down in much the same way as a distorted tin lid can be popped in and out. This inner wall is capable of oscillating at up to 600 times a second, and the noise it produces is greatly amplified by the two resonating chambers contained within the abdomen. Each species has its own distinctive song, and some are so loud that a single insect can be heard as far as 500 metres away.

Assassin Bugs are vicious hunters.

Which insect spends 17 years underground?

A North American Cicada, sometimes known as the Seventeen-year Locust, spends 17 years of its development beneath the soil, extracting sap from roots with its piercing mouthparts. When the adult winged insect emerges, it completes its life cycle high in the trees, where it is frequently preyed on by birds.

Two Scarab Beetles, (Dung Beetles) push a ball of dung to a secure hiding place.

Why do Scarab Beetles roll dung along the ground?

The Scarab Beetles feed on buried dung balls and also lay their eggs in them, covering the dung with a tough skin to prevent the food store and the larvae from drying out. They roll dung balls along the ground in order to find a suitable place to bury them: ideally they like shady places with loose soil to make the work easier.

Why are Assassin Bugs so called?

Assassin Bugs, common throughout the world, derive their name from the speed and ferocity with which they attack and paralyse their prey. All Assassin Bugs have a powerful curved beak which they use to pierce and suck out the juices of their prey, and long powerful forelimbs which they use for grasping.

True Flies and Caddis Flies

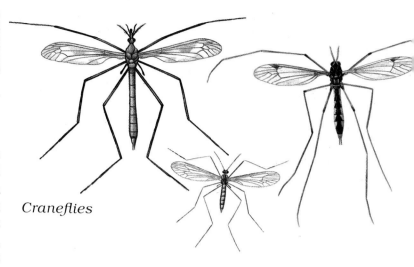

Craneflies

What is a Caddis Fly?

A Caddis Fly is a moth-like insect whose wings are covered with short, fine hairs, not scales, and whose mouthparts are poorly developed. The larva of the Caddis Fly is more familiar to us: living on the pond or river bottom, it makes itself a portable case out of various debris such as leaf fragments, sand and broken stalks – the chosen materials depending on the species. The case is held together by threads of silk, and the larva's soft white body lies protected within it.

What are the feeding habits of the Housefly?

A Housefly will eat practically anything from which nourishment can be obtained – as long as it can be turned into liquid form. This includes all manner of animal and vegetable products – rotten or otherwise – and excrement. The Housefly's mouthparts consist of a proboscis or long sucking tube which is folded beneath its head when not in use. When a Housefly lands on a suitable food, it extends its proboscis over the food and pumps out digestive juices to liquefy and partially digest the food. Liquefied food is then sucked up through the proboscis. The food left behind is contaminated not only by the fly's digestive juices, but also by bacteria which can cause serious diseases.

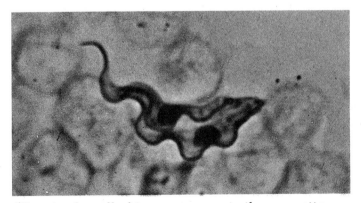

The single-celled trypanosome is the parasite that causes sleeping sickness.

How many wings has a Cranefly?

A Cranefly, like other true flies, has only one pair of wings. The hindwings have become reduced to a pair of club-shaped sticks which during flight whirl around and act as balancing organs. They also detect any deviation from the flight path rather like an automatic pilot in an airplane.

What did Samson mean when he said 'Out of the strong comes forth sweetness'?

This famous riddle was based on Samson's failure to distinguish between a Honeybee and a Dronefly. He saw what he thought were swarms of bees emerging from the dead body of a lion, and reasoned that they could produce honey – hence the riddle. The 'bees', however, were Drone-flies, whose larvae grow and pupate in any decaying organic matter. If he had looked more closely at the 'bees', he would have noticed that they only had one pair of wings and could not sting – a classic case of bee mimicry.

Which fly is the carrier of sleeping sickness?

The Tsetse Fly of tropical Africa, with its specialized blood-sucking mouthparts, transmits the tiny single-celled parasites (*trypanosomes*) which cause sleeping sickness in humans. The female gives birth to no more than 12 larvae in her short six-month lifespan, yet large tracts of land in Africa are considered uninhabitable because of the presence of this fly.

Bees, Wasps and Ants

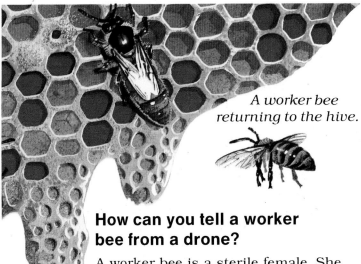

A worker bee returning to the hive.

What is the difference between a wasp and a bee?

Like all insects the bodies of bees and wasps are divided into three parts. Bees though are far more stockily built, with furry bodies, unlike wasps, which usually have sleek, hairless bodies. Bees also gather pollen and produce beeswax and honey, which wasps do not, with the exception of two wasp species found in central America.

How are queen bees produced?

Queen bees are produced from fertilized eggs just the same as worker bees: the secret of their development lies in their diet and the shape of their cell. When the colony senses the need for a new queen, special rounded cells are produced which are much larger than the typical hexagonal comb cells in which worker bees are reared. The queen bee lays normal fertilized eggs in these cells, which hatch after three days and are then fed exclusively on a special, protein-rich substance called 'royal jelly'. Sixteen days later, the new queens start to emerge, five days earlier than a worker bee egg laid at the same time.

A queen bee laying eggs in the comb cells.

How can you tell a worker bee from a drone?

A worker bee is a sterile female. She is produced from a fertilized egg and is fully equipped for gathering nectar, making honey and maintaining the hive. A worker bee is usually between 12 and 15 millimetres long. A drone, however, is a male bee produced from an unfertilized egg. He does nothing to maintain the hive, his sole purpose is to mate with the new queen. Drones tend to be bigger (14–18 millimetres), with broader heads, and are incapable of stinging.

What is the first thing a queen Honeybee does on emerging from her cell?

Her first task is to kill off all the other new queens laid at the same time, to ensure that her supremacy is unchallenged. She does not confront the old queen, however: instead, the old queen prepares to swarm and establish a new nesting site elsewhere, with a band of loyal workers.

How is honey made?

Honey is made from nectar, the sugary liquid present in flowers, which is sucked up by bees using their long tongues and stored in their honey stomachs. When the bee's honey stomach is full, it returns to the hive and passes the nectar to other workers as a thin runny fluid. The hive bees then mix the nectar with secretions from their mouths, before depositing it in open cells in the honeycomb. Within about three days the nectar compound is transformed into honey. The finished honey is then sealed with a wax cap until needed for future use.

Why do bees dance?

Bees perform a 'dance' on the honeycomb to let other bees know where the nectar-rich flowers are to be found. Using the Sun and hive as reference points, a bee will dance in a figure of eight, the orientation of which shows the other bees the direction in which the food lies. The frequency and rapidity with which the bee waggles its abdomen are important clues to the distances involved.

Why do Honeybees collect resin?

Honeybees collect resin from trees to make a varnish-like substance called *propolis*. This substance is used to seal up any small crevices or holes in the hive, and also to cover up any unwanted objects which are too large to be removed.

How does a Potter Wasp care for its young?

Potter Wasps build little pots of clay from fine damp soil and attach them to plants. The female then hunts caterpillars and spiders, and crams this stock of paralysed victims into the pot. The egg is then suspended inside the pot from a thread. In this way the emerging larva is provided with sufficient 'fresh' food to complete its development.

Where does the Ichneumon Wasp lay her eggs?

The Ichneumon Wasp has a long egg-laying tube (*ovipositor*). She listens on the trunk of a conifer tree for the grub of the woodwasp, then she plunges her ovipositor into the wood by the fat grub. Next she lays an egg on the woodwasp grub, which provides a living foodstore for the hatchling ichneumon larva.

How do Honeybees collect pollen?

Honeybees have small depressions on their hind-legs called pollen baskets. When a bee enters a flower tiny hairs on the hindlegs collect pollen from the stamen. The front and middle legs also strip pollen from the flower and pack it into the pollen baskets.

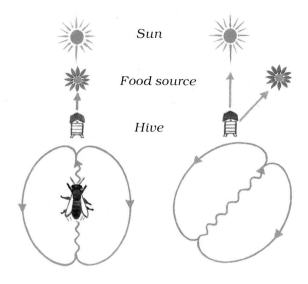

Sun

Food source

Hive

The bee's 'dance' shows other workers where to find the best food supply.

What 'household chores' is a worker bee expected to perform?

During the first three weeks of life, the workers tend to the larvae, feed the queen and the drones. They build and repair the honeycomb using wax secreted from special glands on their abdomens, and venture out on short flights to build up a mental picture of where the hive is in relation to its surroundings.

How does a Honeybee colony differ from that of a Bumblebee?

Honeybees are said to live in permanent communities with the queen leading her colony for two or three years. Bumble-bees occupy their nest sites for one year only; the queen and other colony members die at the end of the summer after the new males and the young queens have been produced.

White-tailed Bumble Bee

Red-tailed Bumble Bee

Honey Bee

What are Cuckoo Bees?

Cuckoo Bees are the insect equivalent of the European Cuckoo bird. They infiltrate the nests of others and substitute their eggs for those of the host species. The *Psithyrus* Cuckoo Bee looks like a Bumblebee, except that it lacks pollen baskets and cannot make wax. The queen Cuckoo Bee will sneak into the nest of a newly-formed Bumblebee colony and hide under the honeycomb until she has acquired the smell of the colony. She then destroys the eggs of the Bumblebee and uses the wax to make her own egg cells. Eventually she will kill the Bumblebee queen and become the sole egg-producer.

What is a nectar thief?

When most insects collect nectar from plants they also carry away pollen, which enables the plant to reproduce. Bumblebees and some other insects, however, are able to 'steal' nectar from certain plants. Some flowers are too long and thin for the insect to reach the nectar with its tongue or proboscis. It will then drill through the flower from the outside and suck out the nectar. The bee therefore takes nectar but does not collect any pollen.

How do ants communicate?

Ants communicate with each other by a process of mutual feeding or 'kissing'. When the ants kiss, they not only pass food to each other, but they also pass secretions which they have picked up from licking the body of the queen, her eggs and her larvae. These secretions also help ants to recognize each other because each colony has its own particular odour. Some ants can also give off alarm secretions from special glands. It is these secretions which enable ants to live in such an organized way.

What is the life cycle of an ant?

Ants pass through three stages before becoming adults: egg, larva, pupa. As the queen lays eggs they are licked clean by the workers and transferred to the 'nursery'. After a few weeks they hatch into helpless larvae, which the worker ants feed. After a while they pupate, spinning silken cocoons in which the larvae are transformed into adults. When they are ready to emerge, the workers often help them out by tearing open the cocoons. Usually the ants that emerge are wingless female workers, but occasionally winged males and females appear which eventually attempt to form their own colonies.

Why are some ants described as farmer ants?

Just as humans tend herds of cows and stimulate the production of milk, so ants 'milk' tiny plant-feeding insects, called aphids, for honeydew. By stroking the aphids with their antennae, the ants make the aphids secrete honeydew. The ants drink and store this in their crops. The ants also look after the aphids by chasing away enemies such as ladybirds and hoverfly grubs.

Which ant grows its own food?

The Leafcutter Ants of Central and South America strip leaves from trees and use them as a basis for growing fungi in their underground 'gardens'. The workers chew the leaves and compress them into fungus beds, fertilizing the growth of the fungus with their droppings. The growing fungus is used to feed the whole colony.

Soldier Ants

OTHER INVERTEBRATES

Is a spider an insect?

Spiders are not insects but *arachnids*. Unlike an insect, which has six legs, a spider has eight legs. Spiders do not have wings, nor do they have antennae, although a pair of slender palps at the front of the head may sometimes be mistaken for these. A spider's body is usually hairy and is divided into two main parts – a combined head and chest, and an abdomen. The two are linked by a narrow waist. All spiders have a pair of poison fangs with which to kill their prey, and all are capable of producing silk, although they don't always use it to make webs.

Unlike an insect, a spider has eight legs.

Why do you find spiders in the bath?

Contrary to popular belief, house spiders do not come up the plughole. They cannot live in water and quickly drown if flushed away. The spider you find in the bath is probably a long-legged male spider which has fallen into the bath. A spider cannot grip on to the bath's slippery surface, so it has little option but to wait until some kindly person helps it out.

How do spiders eat?

Spiders can take food only in liquid form. They do not have proper jaws for chewing, and use the sharp teeth at the base of each fang to chew their prey, pouring digestive juices over it so that the resulting mush is easier to suck up. Crab Spiders, which have no teeth, simply inject digestive juices into their prey, and suck out the contents through a hole, leaving behind an empty husk.

What is an arachnophobe?

Are you afraid of spiders? If you are, then you are an arachnophobe! European spiders are mainly harmless and there is no reason to fear them. There are dangerous spiders living in warmer climates, spiders whose bites can cause severe pain and in some rare cases even death. One of the world's largest and most feared spiders, the South American Bird Spider, is actually not very dangerous to humans. Its bite is no worse than a bee sting.

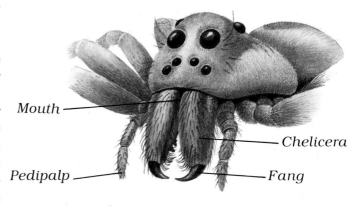

Mouth — Chelicera — Pedipalp — Fang

The mouth parts of a spider

How does a spider make its web?

A spider produces liquid silk from the end of its abdomen. The silk hardens as soon as it is exposed to the air, making a thread stronger than steel wire of the same thickness. The most familiar spider's web is the orb web which is made by many spiders and resembles a bicycle wheel. To make an orb web, the spider first spins a thread between two supports and then lays a slack thread below it, which the spider pulls down to form a 'V' shape. The point of this V-shape will become the centre or 'hub' of the web from which the spider flings out other 'spokes'. It completes the outer rim by attaching more threads to suitable supports and, when all the rim threads and radial spokes are in position, the spider spins a strengthening spiral, moving outwards from the hub to the rim. Finally, starting from the outside, it lays a spiral inwards, using special sticky silk for trapping insects. On reaching the central hub it either takes up a waiting position on a special platform, or goes into hiding nearby.

How does a spider avoid becoming entangled in its own web?

A spider avoids becoming stuck to its own web by using two different threads to construct it. The hub of the web, where the spider may lie in wait, is made of 'dry' threads, as are the 'spokes' of the web, while the rest of the web is made of sticky silk. When the spider scampers across its web, it uses the dry spokes and is careful to avoid touching the sticky threads with its legs. Even if it did, the oily secretions on its feet would prevent it from sticking.

Are spiders dangerous to humans?

Almost all spiders have venom glands which produce poison to subdue their prey. Only one small family of web-spinning spiders manage without such poisons. But the vast majority of spiders cannot hurt human beings with their venom. There are only about 30 species that are really dangerous to us. Many spiders cannot even pierce our skin with their fangs, and most of those that can bite us cause nothing more than pain or itching. The truly dangerous spiders include the notorious Black Widow spider whose venom is fifteen times more deadly than that of a rattlesnake.

How much silk does a spider use in making its web?

A large spider's web can contain 30 metres of silk, silk so fine (a few thousandths of a millimetre thick) that it rarely weighs more than half a milligramme. The web can support a spider 4000 times its own weight – and hold prey weighing much more – a tribute to the excellence of the web's design.

Why must a male spider take care when courting a female?

Extreme caution is required by the male, otherwise he may end up being eaten by the female. To avoid this happening, the male employs various courtship rituals. Male web-making spiders signal to the female by twanging her web in a particular way, while other species may present the female with a silk-wrapped insect, to divert her attention as they mate with her. If the male stays too long, the female may suddenly bite him, wrap him in silk and use his body to provide the nourishment for the eggs.

Female spiders will often eat the males who have come to mate with them.

A Trapdoor Spider in its burrow

How does the Trapdoor Spider capture its prey?

Trapdoor Spiders live in hot tropical regions, in burrows capped with a hinged trapdoor made of silk. The spider sits in its burrow and waits for the vibrations made by a passing prey. It then flips up the door, pounces, drags its victim into the burrow and eats it.

Can spiders fly?

Spiders do not have wings but this does not mean they never take to the air. Young spiders of certain species, in an attempt to get away from their brothers and sisters, will draw a thread of silk from their abdomens and wait for the wind to catch it. This draws more silk from the spider's abdomen, lifting the spider up as the pull of the silk increases. Sometimes the spiders are carried hundreds of kilometres. 'Ballooning', as this method of travel is known, is an efficient way of ensuring that all suitable habitats are colonized by the spiders.

Do all scorpions have a deadly sting?

The sting of a scorpion is located at the tip of its long curved tail, which is either held to one side or arched over the scorpion's back. Some scorpions only have a mild sting, while others, particularly members of the family *Buthidae*, can be deadly to human beings. Scorpions live in hot, dry regions, and are active mainly at night, feeding on spiders, insects and other small animals. They capture their prey using their large pincers, some crushing their victims to death without using their poisonous stings.

Scorpion

Why is a Harvestman sometimes mistaken for a spider?

Long-legged Harvestmen have eight legs like a spider, but there the similarity ends. The Harvestman's body is a single unit, with no obvious waist, and it is incapable of making a web. Its second pair of legs is always longer than the other three pairs, and it only has two simple eyes, unlike the six or eight in a true spider. They are most noticeable around harvest-time, when the adults mature.

Harvestman

Other Arthropods

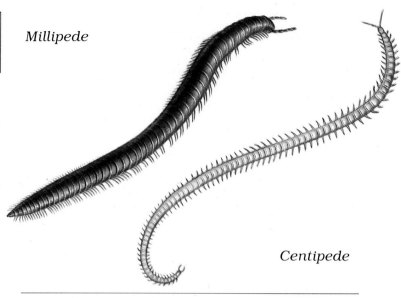

Millipede

Centipede

Do centipedes really have a hundred legs?

Although 'centipede' literally means a hundred feet, no centipede has exactly that number. Some may have more, some less but the most familiar garden centipedes have only 15 pairs of legs. Centipedes prefer to live in dark, damp places, such as under logs and stones.

What is the difference between a centipede and a millipede?

A millipede is usually thought to have more legs than a centipede, but to try and distinguish between them by counting the legs could be confusing. The proper way to tell between a centipede and a millipede is by looking at the number of pairs of legs per body segment. Millipedes have two pairs of legs on most segments, whereas centipedes only have one. Also, a millipede's body is usually rounded in cross-section, whereas a centipede's is flattened. Millipedes tend to be long, slender and slow-moving, feeding off dead vegetable matter in the soil or leaf litter.

Why are millipedes more passionate than centipedes?

Millipedes are strictly vegetarian, so a potential partner never risks being eaten alive. A centipede, which is carnivorous, isn't averse to tucking into a fellow centipede given the chance. Millipedes can therefore entwine themselves when mating in order to make sure sperm is transferred from the male to the female. Centipedes, however, rely on the female picking up a packet of sperm deposited by the male, without the two creatures ever touching.

How often does a sheep-tick eat?

During the three years of a sheep-tick's life, it takes only three meals, spending less than a month attached to its hosts.

Why should you never pull a sheep-tick off your skin?

If a sheep-tick has burrowed into your skin, its mouthparts will be so securely anchored that they will be left behind if the tick is simply plucked off, and will lead to inflammation. Instead, you can either cover the tick with a plaster (which irritates it and causes it to release its hold), or you can smear it with methylated spirit, which also dislodges it.

Is a woodlouse an insect?

The Common Woodlouse is more closely related to crabs than to insects. They have seven pairs of legs, and their bodies are covered with horny, overlapping plates which allow water both in and out. Consequently they seek out dark, damp places to avoid drying out, and are active mainly at night, when the air is cool and humid.

How does a woodlouse shed its skin?

Instead of shedding its skin all at once, a woodlouse moults in two stages. The rear half is lost first. If the animal is discovered at this stage, it looks very peculiar with the front half its normal greyish colour and the remainder a creamy white. Only when the rear hardens and become grey, does the woodlouse shed its front portion. Normally the woodlouse goes into hiding during moulting, because it is vulnerable to predators.

Crabs and Crayfish

Hermit Crab

What is a crustacean?

Crustaceans have sometimes been described as the water-breathing insects of the sea. They do in fact belong to the same order (*Arthropoda*) as insects, and comprise an enormous variety of species, most of which live in the sea. Their chief unifying feature is the possession of two pairs of antennae. Crabs, lobsters, prawns, shrimps, water-fleas and barnacles all belong to this group.

How big is the biggest crustacean?

The Japanese Spider Crab, with an outstretched clawspan of over three metres, qualifies as the largest crustacean in the world. The limbs themselves, which may measure up to two metres in length, are so heavy that its muscles are unable to move them without the support of water. Specimens brought ashore in fishing nets have great difficulty in moving.

Where do crabs live?

Most live in the sea or on the coast, and a few in rivers. In the tropics, some crabs spend a large part of their lives on dry land, and a few species climb trees. There are even rainforest crabs living in tiny pools of water held by plants growing high up on the branches of trees.

Which crabs live on land?

In tropical countries, many Hermit Crabs spend most of their lives on land, adopting empty snail shells as their homes and living on a diet of plant and animal food. The most remarkable and also the largest of these land-living crustaceans, however, is the Robber Crab. Measuring 30 centimetres across the shell, it can encircle a coconut palm trunk with its legs, and easily scales these trees to rob them of their fruit. Like all Hermit Crabs, it returns to the sea to breed.

Which crab makes its home in discarded mollusc shells?

Hermit Crabs have abandoned their own protective armour in favour of that provided by empty mollusc shells. Their soft pink bodies are naturally twisted to fit easily into the coils of their borrowed home. Their claws are uneven, the right one being larger, flattened and more heavily armoured to provide a secure 'door' to the shell. Not only does the thick mollusc shell prevent the Hermit Crab from being eaten by fish, lobsters and octopuses, it also saves it the hazardous task of shedding its shell and growing another one. As a Hermit Crab outgrows its borrowed home, it simply swaps it for a larger one.

How many legs does a crayfish have?

In common with crabs, prawns, lobsters and shrimps, crayfish have ten legs, two pairs of five. The first pair of legs is enlarged to form nippers, while the other four pairs are used for walking. Crayfish are nocturnal scavengers which thrive in fast-moving, freshwater streams, in chalky areas. Their tails and abdomens are considered to be a delicacy.

Why are cooked lobsters red?

Lobsters look fearsome, with their enlarged pincers, but in fact they are scavengers and live off the remains of dead sea creatures. Living lobsters are bluish-black in colour, to blend in with the sea bottom. They become red on cooking due to a chemical change in their pigments.

Which crustacean is vital for the survival of the great whales?

Tiny, shrimp-like krill forms a major part of the diet of many whales, and also of seals, penguins, petrels and many other large marine creatures. These tiny crustaceans form immense shoals of some 100 million individuals in the Antarctic Ocean. In one year alone a Blue Whale may consume up to 450 tonnes of krill. The harvesting of krill by factory fishing fleets may further reduce the whales' chances of survival.

How do barnacles capture their prey?

Barnacles are crustaceans which spend their adult lives firmly fixed in one place – usually on rocks, but also on driftwood, ships and even on other marine creatures. The most common barnacles of the seashore are the Acorn Barnacles. As the incoming tide sweeps over them, six pairs of bristly tentacles are thrust out into the water, to collect any passing food particles. As the tide ebbs, the tentacles are brought in, and the barnacles shut their shells to reduce evaporation.

Which barnacle is a parasite of crabs?

The root-headed barnacle *Sacculina* attaches itself to the body of a young crab and injects a few of its cells into the crab's bloodstream. These float around inside the crab's body and finally settle near the gut, where they absorb nourishment from the crab and send out root-like processes all over the crab's body. The *Sacculina* parasite destroys the crab's reproductive organs and prevents the crab from moulting. Eventually the parasite appears as an egg-filled lump under the crab's abdomen, from where it can leave and attach itself to a new host.

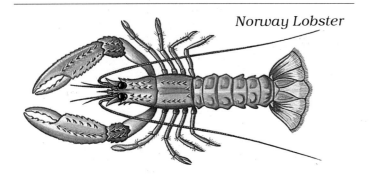

Norway Lobster

Why does the male Fiddler Crab have one enlarged claw?

Fiddler Crabs are common on the mud flats of salt marshes and mangrove swamps in tropical regions. When the tide is out they scuttle about, holding their single enormous claws in the air like large flags. These enlarged claws are brightly coloured, often red, and serve two purposes. Firstly, they are used to threaten other males, warning them off their territory, and secondly, they are used in an elaborate courtship display. The smaller claw is used like a spoon for feeding, scraping green algae and plant debris off the mud.

Crab

Can crabs swim?

Shore crabs have given up swimming altogether, and use all four pairs of legs to propel themselves along in a curious sideways manner. Swimming crabs, however, have modified their fourth pair of legs into a pair of flattened paddles. The crab moves these paddles rapidly up and down in the water, driving itself forward at considerable speed.

Where does scampi come from?

The popular food scampi consists of the tail parts of the Norway Lobster, a small, burrowing crustacean which lives in large numbers at the bottom of the North Sea. It is orange with red markings, and has five pairs of legs, the first pair of which is enlarged to form a pair of nipping claws.

FISHES

What is a fish?

A fish is a vertebrate (animal with a backbone) which spends the whole of its life in water. The body is usually covered in scales, and it has fins which help it to swim through water. Most fish are cold-blooded and extract their oxygen from water by means of gills, which are the equivalent of lungs in air-breathing animals.

How many fish are there?

Fish are by far the most numerous of all vertebrates. There are estimated to be over 22,000 different types of fish, of which about a third live in freshwater and two-thirds in the sea. Scientists classify fish into three groups: jawless fish (of which there are about 60 species); sharks and rays (about 600 species); and bony fish (over 20,000 species). The bony fish are without doubt the most successful and have colonized almost every body of water on Earth.

Why do fish die if taken out of water?

Like all animals, fish need oxygen to live. Unlike land-living animals, fish can only take in oxygen if it is dissolved in water. When a fish is removed from water, it is removed from its source of dissolved oxygen and soon dies if not put back. Fish gulp in water through their mouths, forcing it over their pink gills and out through openings on either side of the head.

Why are freshwater snails important to pond fish?

A healthy pond is a self-contained community of plants and animals, all living together in natural harmony. However, if something happens to upset this balance, then the whole community can be put at risk. For instance, freshwater snails help to keep the plants under control, and so maintain the balance of gases in the water. Without them, plant growth would proceed unchecked, depleting the water of oxygen. Fish cannot survive without oxygen, and within a short while, the pond would be choked with weeds and devoid of all animal life.

What is a bony fish?

A fish is described as being bony if its skeleton is made of bone and its body is covered in overlapping scales. Its gills are usually protected by a bony flap of skin and it usually has a swimbladder. Bony fish thrive in both fresh- and saltwater, and come in a great variety of shapes and sizes.

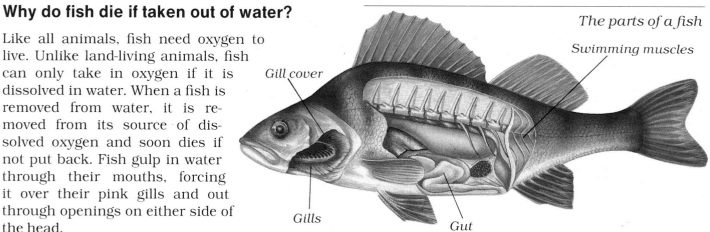

The parts of a fish

Swimming muscles

Gill cover

Gills

Gut

How can you tell the age of a fish?

Unlike land-living animals, which stop growing when they reach maturity, fish keep on growing throughout their lives. The older a fish is, the bigger it is. And because the number of scales covering the fish's body remain constant, they too increase in size as the fish grows, forming tell-tale growth rings from which the age of the fish can be calculated.

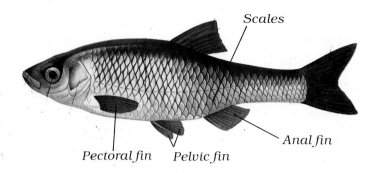

Scales

Anal fin

Pectoral fin   Pelvic fin

The position of the fins on a fish's body

How do fish swim?

Most fish swim using a side-to-side movement of their bodies, the thrust forward being powered by a wave of muscular contraction spreading down the body. The strong muscles which run down either side of the fish's body may sometimes account for up to 75 per cent of the fish's weight, and are often the part of the fish we like to eat.

What role do fins play in swimming?

The fins on most bony fish do not propel the fish through the water: their role is more concerned with manoeuvring, helping the fish to steer a straight and steady course through the water. Each fin has a specific job to do. The paired pectoral and pelvic fins control pitching up and down, and act as brakes when the fish wants to stop moving forwards. The single dorsal and anal fins keep the fish upright, preventing it from rolling from side to side, while the tail fin acts as an efficient and well-designed rudder.

What is a shoal?

A shoal is a collection of fish which live together. The shape can vary from species to species, herring form ribbon-like shoals sometimes several miles long. Others, such as the Californian Sardine, may rush together to form a compact ball if startled. Commercial fisheries rely heavily on the fact that fish form shoals – it is far easier to catch large numbers of densely grouped fish than scattered individuals.

Why do fish shoal?

Fish shoal chiefly because there is safety in numbers. Shoaling fish have been seen to baffle a predator by encircling it and then following behind it, the members of the shoal co-ordinating their movements with astonishing precision. It is just possible that the predator was hoodwinked into thinking that the shoal was one huge fish, and decided to leave well alone!

A shoal of fish

How do fish in shoals avoid bumping into each other?

Fish possess a system for sensing movement in the water around them. It is called the *lateral line* system, and consists of a fluid-filled canal running just below the surface of the fish's body, often seen as a textured line. This system enables the fish to detect changes in water pressure caused by the movements of other fish – it is like feeling other fish without touching them.

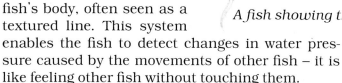

Lateral line

A fish showing the lateral line running down the side of the body.

Do fish sleep?

Although fish cannot close their eyes because they have no eyelids, they do sleep, often resting on the bottom or near water plants. One species of fish, the Parrot Fish, wraps itself in a blanket of mucus before going to sleep, sometimes spending an hour each evening preparing its bed of slime.

How does a fish use its swimbladder?

A swimbladder is simply an air-filled pouch inside the fish's body which acts as a float. Not all fish have swimbladders, but those that do use them to keep afloat in water.

Why do fish lay so many eggs?

Fish lay large numbers of eggs because the chance of each one surviving to adulthood is very small. The majority of fish lay tens of thousands of eggs, then have nothing more to do with them, and many eggs are eaten before they even hatch out. Those fish that do exercise some form of parental care, such as the seahorse and stickleback, tend to lay fewer eggs.

What do fish eat?

Even though most fish are carnivorous (flesh-eaters), all life in the sea ultimately depends on plants. Floating on or near the surface of the water, millions of tiny plants called algae or diatoms form the diet of many small animals such as the crustaceans. These crustaceans are eaten by small fish, which in turn are eaten by larger fish, creating a *food chain* of animals and plants. It is important that the balance of this food chain is maintained: if the number of one particular fish is reduced, for example, by overfishing, it can have far-reaching effects on the rest of the chain.

The biggest fish in the world: the Whale Shark

Which is the biggest fish?

The biggest living fish is the Whale Shark, which can reach lengths of up to 18 metres. It is a filter feeder, feeding on small fish and plankton.

Fish Without Jaws

Why do scientists find jawless fish so interesting?

Jawless fish are a small group of fish consisting of hagfish and lampreys. They are interesting to scientists because they are very simple vertebrates whose ancestors are thought to have given rise to the first true fish. Their long, eel-like bodies lack any limbs, scales, skull or true bones and, like the first fish, they have no jaws.

How do fish without jaws feed?

Hagfish and lampreys both feed through sucker-like mouths, although their feeding habits are quite different. Hagfish use their rasping tongues to bore their way into weak or dead fish, devouring all the flesh to leave just skin and bones behind. Lampreys, on the other hand, have a parasitic lifestyle. They use their suckers, which are lined with sharp, horny teeth to attach themselves to other fish and feed on the host's blood.

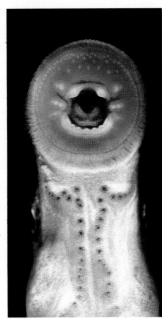

The sucker-like mouth of a lamprey

A lamprey feeding off the flesh of a Brown Trout.

How does the lamprey breathe when it is feeding?

Lampreys normally breathe by pumping water through their mouths, over their gills, and out through their gill openings on either side of the head. However, when the sucker is in action, water has to both enter and pass out through the gill openings.

Why are hagfish so slimy?

The skin of a hagfish is dotted all over with mucus-secreting glands and it is this mucus which makes them particularly slimy to touch. Scientists think this slime helps hagfish to kill their prey more quickly as well as acting as a protective coat.

Where do lampreys lay their eggs?

Adult lampreys live in both salt and freshwater, but all lampreys swim to freshwater to breed. They lay large numbers of eggs in gravel nests, where the eggs hatch into blind burrowing larvae. The larvae live in the muddy beds of streams for up to six years, feeding on tiny plants. It is not until they develop into adults and swim to the sea that their diet changes to blood.

Sharks and Rays

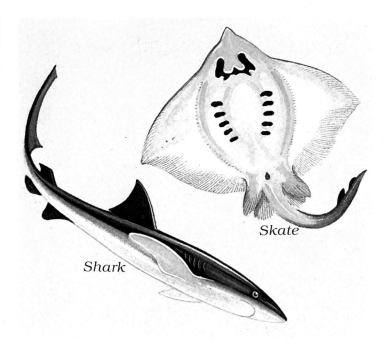

Skate

Shark

How do sharks and rays differ from bony fish?

Sharks and rays live only in the sea and differ from other fish in having a skeleton made of gristle called cartilage. This gristle is similar to bone but more rubbery and not so hard. Their skin is rough, like sandpaper, and they have no protective flap over their gills, making their gill slits easy to see. Perhaps the most important difference is the absence of a swimbladder; sharks and rays have to keep swimming to keep afloat, otherwise they sink to the sea bed.

Are all sharks dangerous?

There are at least 250 species of shark in the world and of these, only about 25 are considered dangerous to human beings. These include the Great White Shark, the Hammerhead Shark, the Tiger Shark and Mako Shark. The largest of these, the Great White Shark, has a fearsome reputation, having been involved in many attacks on humans. Tropical beaches in areas known to be frequented by sharks are often protected by shark nets out at sea.

Thresher Shark

Hammerhead Shark

How do you attract a shark?

Scientists who want to observe sharks in the wild use a simple method of attracting them: they merely lower a piece of meat tied to a rope over the side of a boat. If there are any sharks in the area, then their keen sense of smell soon brings them homing in to the bait. Underwater photographers film the sharks from inside specially built cages.

Why do Hammerhead Sharks have such curiously shaped heads?

Hammerhead Sharks are aggressive, predatory fish, with eyes and nostrils located at each end of their T-shaped heads. Nobody knows for sure what the advantages of such a head shape are. One suggestion is that as the shark swings its head from side to side, it is able to sample the smells from a much wider area than if its eyes and nostrils were closer together.

Great White Shark

How many sets of teeth has a shark?

A shark may have as many as five sets of teeth, set in rows one behind the other. As the teeth in front, along the outside of the jaw are lost or wear out, the teeth behind move forward and replace them. This process of tooth renewal continues throughout the shark's life. As the shark grows in size, so the new teeth tend to be bigger than the ones they replace. Not all shark's teeth look the same and a species can be identified by the shape of its teeth. The teeth of the Great White Shark are triangular with a serrated edge like a saw; the Sand Shark's teeth are more dagger-like.

Why is the Giant Manta also called a Devil Ray?

You only have to look at this fish to guess why! With large flapping 'wings' (which are really huge pectoral fins) spanning over six metres, it glides effortlessly through the water like some ghostly bird. Seamen thought this sinister-looking fish was a harbinger of doom, and pearl divers were afraid that they would be smothered by the ray's wings. They need not have worried, for Giant Mantas are harmless to humans. They feed mainly on plankton and small crustaceans.

The Manta Ray can grow to seven metres across but is harmless to humans. It is a filter feeder and eats only tiny plankton.

How do Thresher Sharks use their tails to capture their prey?

The tail of a Thresher Shark is as long as the rest of its body, and it uses it as a whip to herd shoaling fish into a dense mass before striking. It can also stun individual fish with its tail.

What is the best thing to do if you are in the water and you see a shark approaching?

Stay calm! If you can't get out of the water quickly, then try not to appear afraid. Hit the shark with anything that comes to hand, and make a lot of noise. Your chances of survival are greater if you strike a shark before it strikes you.

Why are sharks so drab?

Unlike bony fish, which can see in colour, a shark perceives its world in various shades of grey. This is because almost all sharks lack cone cells (colour receptors) in their eyes. Because they cannot see in colour, there is little point in them having colourful bodies.

How do rays breathe?

Rays are flat-bodied, bottom-dwelling sharks, whose diet consists of molluscs and crustaceans which they grub up from the sea floor. Because their mouths are on the underside of their bodies, the gills would soon become clogged with mud and sand if they took in water by this route. So instead they have two holes, or spiracles, just behind each eye on the upperside of their bodies, through which water is drawn in and passed over the gills.

Freshwater Fish

Why do salmon leap up waterfalls?

Salmon have been known to leap as high as three metres in their efforts to return upstream to their breeding grounds. The salmon is a remarkable fish. The mature adult, having spent several years at sea feeding and growing, returns to the river or stream in which it was born to breed. Once breeding has finished many salmon die, their bodies wasted and exhausted by the journey.

How do salmon find their way back to their birthplace?

Nobody knows for sure how salmon find their way home, although there is some evidence to suggest that the fish rely partly on smell to guide them back. It may be that the smell of the stream in which the salmon was born becomes indelibly imprinted on its brain. Salmon are also thought to have an in-built compass, which they use together with the position of the sun and the stars to navigate home across the oceans.

Does the Four-eyed Fish really have four eyes?

The Four-eyed Fish of Central America in fact has only two eyes, but because they project well above the head and are divided into two parts, they act as four. The two lower halves are for seeing underwater, and the two upper halves for seeing in air. As the fish swims along at the surface of the water, it is able to see prey both in the air and in the water at the same time.

The Mudskipper can breathe air.

Salmon jumping a waterfall on their way upstream to spawn.

Which fish can give you an electric shock?

The Electric Eel is one of the few animals in the world that kills its prey by electrocution and can produce shocks of up to 500 volts. Electric Eels live in the black, oxygen-poor rivers of the Amazon basin and rely not on vision to find their way about but on electricity. They send out small electric pulses which rebound off objects in the water to give the eel an 'electric picture' of the world about it.

Which fish breathes air?

Warm, stagnant water has very little oxygen in it, and to survive in these conditions certain fish have developed a type of lung. The African Lungfish has poorly developed gills, and regularly gulps air at the water surface, 'swallowing' it into a pair of simple lungs through an opening in its throat. The walls of these lungs, developed from the swim bladder, are thickly lined with blood vessels which absorb the oxygen, enabling the lungfish to survive for long periods in difficult conditions.

How fierce are piranha fish?

The ferocity of the piranha fish is legendary. Its razor-sharp jaws are operated by huge muscles and are lined with large, pointed triangular teeth. These fearsome jaws are capable of chopping out a piece of flesh with the precision of a razor. Unlike most predatory fish, piranha hunt in shoals, and their aggressive behaviour is thought to be linked to the breeding season, when males are guarding the eggs. Piranha are found in the streams and rivers of South America, and are attracted to any disturbance or hint of blood in the water. One reliable record tells of a 45-kilogram rodent such as an agouti being stripped to a skeleton in less than a minute.

The teeth of the ferocious Piranha.

Which fish takes its name from a heavyweight boxer?

Once a popular aquarium fish, the Jack Dempsey is so aggressive that it was named after the American boxer who held the world heavyweight title from 1919 to 1926. These colourful fish grow to quite a large size, and are easy to breed in captivity.

Which fish is a crackshot?

The Archer Fish has the unusual ability to shoot down insects and other small creatures that land on waterside plants. The fish will squirt drops of water from its mouth, like pellets from an airgun. The pellets hit unsuspecting insects, knocking them from their perches into the water. Adult Archer Fish can hit insects that are as much as 1.5 metres away.

A pike feeding on another fish.

Why does the pike have such a bad reputation?

The Northern Pike is a renowned predator of still waters and sluggish rivers, although many claims about its size and ferocity are grossly exaggerated. Equipped with long, hooked teeth, pike lurk among water weeds, ready to dart out and snatch up any passing fish. They even eat small birds and mammals. Large individuals may weigh as much as 23 kilograms.

Why does the Splashing Tetra splash water at leaves?

This South American fish lays its eggs out of water to escape the attentions of predatory fish. The female leaps out of the water and clings on to a leaf just long enough to lay some eggs, then the male leaps out and fertilizes them. The male stays underneath the eggs for about three days splashing them to keep them moist until they hatch and drop into the water.

Which fish makes its nest from bubbles?

The male Siamese Fighting Fish is one of several fish which builds its nest out of sticky bubbles. As the female sheds her eggs, they are fertilized by the male who then catches them and spits them into the nest. The male guards the nest and replaces the bubbles as necessary until the young hatch out.

Siamese Fighting Fish

How does the stickleback build its nest?

The male stickleback builds his nest using small pieces of water plants, gluing them together with a sticky secretion from his kidneys. Once he has assembled a small heap, he then burrows through the middle to make a tunnel, thereby completing the nest. Displaying a bright red belly, the male entices a female into the nest to lay eggs. The male stickleback guards the nest until the eggs hatch and the young are ready to leave. The males do not learn this behaviour but all perform exactly the same actions.

Can the Climbing Perch climb trees?

Ever since 1791 when it was discovered up a palm tree by the Danish naturalist, Daldorff, its name has stuck, even though the fish are rarely found in trees. This large Asian fish has a special 'labyrinth organ' which enables it to breathe air. Should its home show signs of drying up it can haul itself out of the water and 'walk' across land in search of a new home. It walks using its pectoral fins as props and pushing forward using determined wriggling movements of its tail.

Which fish can fly?

The South American Common Hatchetfish and its related species are the only fish in the world known to use powered flight (as opposed to gliding). Its long pectoral fins act like wings, and you can hear them beating noisily when the fish is airborne. The hatchetfish rarely flies farther than two metres and flies only when threatened.

The Marbled (top) *and Common* (above) *Hatchet fish*

Which fish hatches its eggs in its mouth?

Many of the African cichlid fish, a family of tropical freshwater fish, carry their eggs in their mouths to protect them from predators. The female Nile Mouthbrooder, for example, broods her eggs in her mouth until they are ready to hatch, when she appears to give birth by spitting. Even after the young have hatched they stay close to the mother, returning to the safety of her mouth when predators threaten.

Sticklebacks lay eggs in a nest, built by the male.

Marine Fish

Why is the Coelacanth called a living fossil?

Coelacanths are large, heavy-bodied fish which were thought to have died out 70 million years ago. When a living coelacanth was caught off the coast of South Africa in 1938, it was as if someone had discovered a living dinosaur! Living coelacanths bear close similarities to their fossilized ancestors. Their lobed fins have fleshy bases which look like the beginnings of limbs, and they are known to give birth to fully-formed live young. Scientists believe that some of the first vertebrates to live on land looked like coelacanths.

Why does the Remora fish hitch a ride on a shark?

The Remora is a fish which hates being by itself, and will attach itself to sharks or to any other suitably large fish. It sticks itself on by means of a ridged disc on the top of its head, which acts as a suction pad. As it hitches a ride, the Remora benefits from any scraps of food left over by the shark. In return it rids the shark of any parasites living on its skin.

Which fish swim on their sides?

All species of flatfish swim on their sides. Their flattened bodies have twisted themselves around in such a way that one side becomes the back or upperside and the other side the lower or 'blind' side. The bones of the skull twist so that both eyes fall on the upperside, and in some species the mouth turns up too. The back of the flatfish typically becomes heavily pigmented, the blind side remaining pale or white. Flatfish tend to be bottom-dwellers, and are usually well camouflaged.

The Coelacanth, thought to be extinct until 1938.

Do Flying Fish really fly?

Flying Fish do not fly but glide through the air using their enlarged pectoral fins (and sometimes pelvic fins too) as wings. Just before take-off, a Flying Fish swims rapidly towards the surface until the front part of its body is lifted clear. It then gives a 'kick' with the extra-large lower lobe of its tail fin and, spreading its fins, takes to the air. A Flying Fish may glide as far as 90 metres and can rise as much as 1.5 metres above the water surface.

Which is the most poisonous fish?

Not only is the Stonefish the most poisonous fish in the world, it is also one of the ugliest. It is found in the shallow tropical waters of southern Asia and northern Australia where its rough, warty skin and drab, mottled colouring make it extremely difficult to see. Its huge venom glands are located at the base of each of its 13 dorsal fin spines; anyone unfortunate enough to tread on these spines receives a deadly and excruciatingly painful wound.

The poisonous Stonefish

The Seahorse is a fish but a poor swimmer.

In which group of fish does the male have a pouch for carrying the eggs?

The seahorses and some pipefish. In the seahorses, the female has a long egg-laying organ which is used to place the eggs in the male's pouch. The tiny young seahorses leave the pouch about five weeks after the eggs were laid. The male seahorse can care for up to three broods every year, with as many as 50 eggs in each brood.

Why is the Bluefish so vicious?

The Bluefish is a particularly voracious predator, so vicious that it actually kills more than it can eat. In the summer along the coast of the eastern United States, shoals of Bluefish will herd shoals of Menhaden Fish into shallow bays before slaughtering them in a maddened feeding frenzy. Within a short space of time the water becomes bloodied, and a trail of dead and dying fish remain.

How does the Porcupine Fish respond to danger?

Normally a Porcupine Fish swims with the long sharp spines which cover its back lying flat. At the first hint of danger, it inflates its body by gulping water into its stomach, causing its spines to stick out. It looks like a giant pincushion.

What is so unusual about the Ocean Sunfish?

The Ocean Sunfish is quite unlike any other fish and can grow to a huge size, one specimen was four metres long. When viewed from the side, it appears to be almost circular in shape, consisting of a massive head and a curious frilly tail fin. Its mouth is relatively small for so large a fish, and it feeds mainly on jellyfish. It also lays vast numbers of eggs, one female sunfish is known to have contained 300 million eggs!

Can you eat the Death Puffer fish?

Yes, you can, but only if it has been prepared by a specially trained cook, as its eggs, blood and internal organs contain a deadly poison. The flesh is regarded as a great delicacy in Japan, but if it is contaminated by any of the fish's toxic organs it will probably kill anyone who eats it.

Why is the meat of tuna fish dark, and that of flatfish white?

Tuna fish are powerful swimmers, whose muscles are well supplied with blood vessels to fuel them over long distances. Slow-moving flatfish, however, have less need of such a blood supply, and their flesh is consequently paler.

What fish do commercial fishermen catch?

In the past, mainly sea fish that swim in large shoals such as herring, cod, anchovies and tuna. With these huge shoals, the fishermen can easily net a great many fish at once. The other type of fish that have long been caught by fishing boats are the bottom-dwelling 'flatfish' such as plaice, turbot, sole, and halibut. These are caught by trawling a net along the seabed. Modern fishing boats use new methods, such as gill nets, which form a 'wall of death' catching any passing fish. Other ships have lights to attract fish which are then sucked out of the sea by a device like a vacuum cleaner. With these new methods, a greater variety of fish are caught, but not all are edible and many fish are killed for no reason.

Deep-sea Fish

What is life like for a deep-sea fish?

The world of the deep-sea fish is black and cold. Beyond a depth of 750 metres, no sunlight filters through, so no plants are able to grow. Food is scarce, and deep-sea fish have to rely on other animals for their food. To cope with these difficult conditions, deep-sea fish have evolved special mechanisms, which give them strange and often frightening appearances. Most tend to have huge gaping mouths lined with razor-sharp teeth and some have developed light-producing organs which they use to both attract mates and lure prey.

How did the Deep-sea Angler Fish get its name?

Because it goes fishing! Living in total darkness at depths of up to 4000 metres, this ferocious-looking fish is equipped with both fishing rod and luminous bait. The 'fishing rod' on its nose has a swelling at the end which glows brightly in the dark and attracts potential prey. As soon as the victim draws near, the Angler Fish opens its terrible jaws and sucks the prey in.

How does the Gulper Eel manage to swallow such large prey?

Its secret lies in its enormous jaws and elastic stomach. This black eel-like creature stuffs all manner of prey into its mouth, and then forces it into its stretchy stomach. After a heavy meal, a Gulper Eel's body may be so distorted in shape that it has to rest on the ocean floor until the large meal is digested.

How do lanternfish recognize each other in the dark?

There are over 200 species of deep-sea lanternfish and like many other deep-sea fish, they possess numerous light-producing organs on their bodies. The arrangement of these *photopores* differs not only between species but also between the sexes, helping males and females to identify each other in the dark.

Which male fish becomes a parasite of the female?

The male Deep-sea Angler Fish is tiny in comparison to the female. His sole purpose in life is to seek out a female and attach himself to her. He bores into her flesh and their bodies literally become fused, the male receiving all his nourishment from the female's circulatory system. By allowing the male to become a benign parasite, the female Angler Fish's eggs are guaranteed fertilization.

Two of the strange fish that inhabit the ocean depths, the Gulper Eel (below) and (bottom) the Deep-sea Angler Fish.

REPTILES and AMPHIBIANS

What is an amphibian?

An amphibian can be thought of as the half-way stage between a reptile and a fish. Most amphibians spend the first part of their life in water and the adult phase on dry land. They have soft, moist skin and lay their eggs in water or very damp surroundings. They live in wet places, such as swamps and marshes, although they cannot survive in the sea.

How do reptiles differ from amphibians?

Unlike amphibians, reptiles have solved the problem of water loss from their bodies by developing a dry, scaly, watertight skin. Their eggs are protected from the drying effects of the sun and wind by being enclosed in a leathery or parchment-like shell. Reptiles are therefore able to lay their eggs on dry land. Consequently, they have managed to spread to most corners of the Earth. They thrive in the hot deserts but cannot survive the freezing temperatures found at both the poles.

How many amphibians are there?

Compared to fish, reptiles, birds and mammals, the total number of living amphibian species is rather small. Some 2300 species are known, and these can be divided into three groups: frogs and toads (amphibians without tails); newts and salamanders (amphibians with tails); and caecilians (burrowing, limbless amphibians confined to the tropics).

How many reptiles are there?

The 6000 species of reptiles living today are the survivors of an age when reptiles dominated life on this planet. Of the 16 or 17 different groups known to have existed, only four remain: turtles and tortoises; crocodiles and alligators; snakes and lizards; and one reptile in a group of its own, the tuatara.

How do amphibians breathe?

Amphibians use a variety of methods to breathe. During the larval or tadpole stage, most amphibians breathe through their gills, which are later replaced by lungs as the larvae mature into adults. Adult amphibians breathe through both their lungs and their skin, because their lungs are rather simple and weak. Some amphibians spend all their lives in water and retain their larval gills. One group of salamanders, known as the lungless salamanders, have no lungs at all and rely solely on their skins to breathe.

An axolotl

How long do reptiles live?

Most reptiles die before they are 20 years old. Some crocodiles can live as long as human beings, and the Giant Tortoise is reputed to live 200 years.

Do cold-blooded animals really have cold blood?

Many cold-blooded animals manage to achieve a body temperature approaching that of mammals. Some lizards can even maintain temperatures a couple of degrees hotter. The term 'ectothermic' can be applied to all animals which rely on their external surroundings to warm up their bodies. Reptiles and amphibians are ectothermic and are unable to generate and regulate their own body heat.

Are there any advantages in being cold-blooded?

The main advantage of being cold-blooded, or ectothermic, is that you can go for long periods without any food. Some big snakes have been known not to eat for a whole year without any ill effects. This is because they need less energy than birds and mammals to keep alive. When conditions are unfavourable ectothermic animals become inactive, their body temperature falls, their heart rate slows, and a long gap separates each breath.

Baby turtles hatching from their eggs.

Why are reptiles' eggs rarely coloured?

Unlike birds' eggs, which are patterned and coloured as a means of identification and camouflage, all reptiles' eggs are white. Since most reptiles bury their eggs, there is no need for coloration.

What is a tuatara?

A tuatara looks like a large lizard, but is in fact a unique reptile. It is the only survivor of a widespread group of reptiles that arose some 200 million years ago, and flourished before the dinosaurs. It is a stocky, strongly built animal with a large head and primitive backbone, and sluggish movements. It survives only on a few remote islands off New Zealand, where its presence is not threatened by rats.

Tuatara

Frogs and Toads

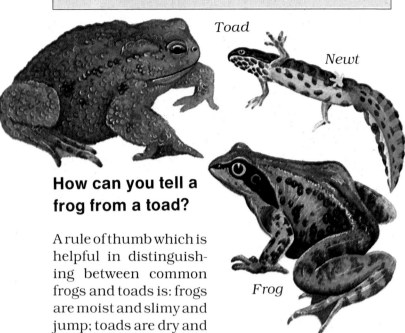

Toad

Newt

Frog

How can you tell a frog from a toad?

A rule of thumb which is helpful in distinguishing between common frogs and toads is: frogs are moist and slimy and jump; toads are dry and warty and walk. However, not all frogs and toads obey this rule: in some parts of the world there are dry, warty frogs and moist, slimy toads.

What is the difference between frog spawn and toad spawn?

Frogs lay their eggs in a mass of protective cloudy jelly, while toad spawn is long and stringy and is typically wound round water plants. The jelly enveloping both types of egg protects the eggs from predators. It also acts as a greenhouse, trapping the sun's warmth and speeding up the eggs' development.

How did the Midwife Toad get its name?

The European Midwife Toad is named after the unusual breeding habits of the male. The male

winds strings of fertilized eggs around his hind legs, and carries them with him all the time, moistening them with occasional visits to a pool. When they are ready to hatch, he returns to the water, where the tadpoles emerge and swim away.

What do frogs and toads eat?

All frogs and toads are flesh-eaters during the adult stage and, as a rule, eat only living prey. Their diet is usually made up of insects, spiders, slugs and worms, although some larger frogs, notably the Horned Frogs and Bullfrogs, are capable of eating small mammals and other amphibians. Most frogs and toads have long, sticky tongues which can be flicked out to catch any unsuspecting prey.

How do tadpoles turn into frogs?

When tadpoles first hatch out, they bear little resemblance to their parents. Breathing through gills and swimming by means of fish-like tails, these tiny black creatures are strictly vegetarian. Eight weeks later their hind legs have appeared, followed soon afterwards by their front legs. At 12 weeks their tails have shrunk, lungs have developed in place of gills, and their heads are decidedly frog-like. Finally the tiny frog crawls out on to land, although it will be three years before it becomes a mature adult.

Which frog gets smaller as it turns into an adult?

The Paradoxical Frog of South America is a most remarkable frog in that it starts life as a huge tadpole – some three times larger than the adult – and then shrinks to a tiny frog as it matures. Even its heart and gut seem to shrink, although no-one seems to know what the possible advantages are.

Which frogs hatch out of their father's mouth?

One of the strangest ways of looking after young is that practised by the male Darwin's Frog, found in southern Chile. Each female lays 20–40 eggs on damp ground and these are then guarded by several males for up to 20 days, until the eggs start to wriggle. Each male then gathers up 10–15 eggs on his tongue and slides them into his voluminous vocal sacs, where they develop. The eggs go through a brief tadpole stage inside the father's mouth before changing into miniature adults.

Which frog will drown if dropped in water?

Unlike most other frogs, the Southern African Rain Frog does not lay its eggs in water. Spending most of its life underground in dry, savannah areas, this fat-looking frog only comes to the surface when it is raining. This frog can neither jump nor swim: if dropped in water it will drown, unless it blows up its body and floats to land.

Do frogs climb trees?

A surprising number of frogs (some 500 species) spend their lives in the tree tops. They are usually small, slender and brightly coloured, with special suction pads at the ends of their toes to enable them to climb trees and cling firmly to branches and leaves. Often described as miniature acrobats, these agile and graceful creatures live mainly in the tropics, although a few, such as the European Tree Frog, can withstand colder climates.

How does the Common Toad defend itself against a snake?

If the toad has no means of escape from the snake, it will try to bluff its way out of trouble. It will stand on tiptoes, straightening its legs, puff up its body and lean menacingly towards the snake. The apparent increase in size of the toad's body may well put the snake off.

Why are some South American Tree Frogs so colourful?

South American Tree Frogs are typically very brightly coloured to warn predators that they are extremely poisonous to eat. All amphibians have mucous glands in their skin to keep them moist. In some frogs these glands also produce a poison so lethal that it can paralyse a bird or monkey almost instantly. South American Indians use secretions from Golden Arrow Poison Frogs to lace the tips of their hunting arrows.

A colourful South American Tree Frog

How does the Surinam Toad care for its young?

The Surinam Toad shows a remarkable degree of parental care. During mating, the skin on the female's back starts to swell and the male then pushes the fertilized eggs on to the female's back. There they stick and become embedded in the spongy tissue, each egg developing in its own separate chamber, until they hatch three months later.

What are the Hairy Frog's hairs used for?

The hairs of the Hairy Frog of west Africa are not hairs at all but threads of skin which appear as a 'frill' on the male during the breeding season. These threads act like an extra set of gills, increasing the surface area over which oxygen and carbon dioxide can be exchanged.

How do Flying Frogs fly?

Flying Frogs don't actually fly but glide between trees. Wallace's Flying Frog of south-east Asia is a highly specialized frog capable of gliding over 15 metres from one tree to another. With extra skin flaps fringing its fore and hind limbs, and enlarged webbed feet, this slender-boned frog looks like a living parachute as it sails through the air. Its large eyes point forwards to help it judge distances between trees.

Newts and Salamanders

What is the difference between a newt and a salamander?

Both newts and salamanders have long cylindrical bodies, long tails and two pairs of equally developed, though often feeble, legs. Salamanders tend to be larger and spend less time in the water than newts. Salamanders are sometimes mistaken for lizards, but their rounded heads and smooth skins (as opposed to the lizard's pointed head and scaly skin) are a sure way to tell the two animals apart.

Marbled Newt

Warty Newt

Palmate Newt

Female Smooth Newt

Types of Newt (above) *and Salamander* (right)

Which amphibian never grows up?

The Mexican Axolotl is often referred to as the Peter Pan of the amphibian world, for it rarely develops into an adult. Remaining in water for the whole of its life, it has managed to sidestep the adult stage, and breeds as a larva or tadpole. If, however, the water it is living in dries up, it develops into the adult form which has lungs.

How can you tell a male newt from a female?

During the breeding season, male newts put on their finery: their colours become brighter, and they develop a crest of skin along their backs. Alpine Newts, Crested Newts and Smooth Newts all display this difference between the sexes.

Why did people think that salamanders were born in fires?

Fire Salamanders are a very brightly coloured amphibian that lives in or under damp pieces of wood. In ancient times people would throw these logs on the fire and, to escape, the salamander would crawl out. It was thought that the animals had been born in the flames. The vivid colorations are to warn other animals that the fire salamander is poisonous.

Male Smooth Newt

Tadpole

Egg

Fire Salamander

Spectacled Salamander

Why is the Olm known as the 'doubtful amphibian'?

The Olm is one of the strangest amphibians known and for a long time scientists didn't know whether to classify it as a fish or an amphibian. Living in underground caves, these blind, pale, eel-like creatures with short, thin legs spend the whole of their lives in water, never passing out of the larval stage. Like the Mexican Axolotl, they never lose their feathery gills.

Tortoises and Turtles

Herman's Tortoise

Pond Terrapin

Where do tortoises and turtles live?

Turtles and tortoises both belong to the same group of reptiles known as *chelonians*, but whereas tortoises live on land, turtles live in the sea. Those chelonians that live in freshwater are called Terrapins or Pond Tortoises.

Why does the African Pancake Tortoise have a soft, flat shell?

The African Pancake Tortoise doesn't retreat into its shell when frightened, instead it rushes into the nearest rock crevice and puffs up its body making it extremely difficult to remove. If it falls when clambering over rocks it can easily right itself because of its flat shell and flexible limbs.

Why do tortoises move so slowly?

Tortoises have no need to move quickly because they carry their armour around with them! At the first hint of danger they withdraw their heads and limbs into their shells until it is safe for them to come out again. Their slow life-style also means that they can keep going while using only a small amount of energy.

Why does the Green Turtle travel hundreds of kilometres to lay her eggs?

Green Turtles feed in warm coastal waters all over the world, yet at nesting time will travel hundreds of kilometres to lay their eggs on the beach where they themselves were born. Turtles feeding off the coast of Brazil will travel over 2000 kilometres to the lonely island of Ascension in the middle of the Atlantic Ocean to lay their eggs. This is because South America was once joined to Africa and as the continents slowly drifted apart, so the gap between Ascension Island and the coast of Brazil grew bigger. The turtles continue to make the journey there and back to this day.

How did Box Tortoises get their name?

Turtle and tortoise shells come in two parts: an upper, domed part (the carapace), and an underneath part (the plastron). In American Box Tortoises, the plastron is hinged, allowing the tortoise to shut itself up completely in a 'box' when danger threatens.

Where does tortoiseshell come from?

Tortoiseshell is widely used as a decorative inlay on furniture and for making jewellery. It is obtained from the Hawksbill Turtle which lives in warm tropical waters. The Hawksbill's bony shell is covered with hard, overlapping scales from which tortoiseshell is made.

How does the Alligator Snapping Turtle capture its prey?

The Alligator Snapping Turtle of North America is the biggest of all freshwater turtles (growing to 90 centimetres). It lies in wait at the bottom of muddy, slow-moving rivers with its jaws open. Attached to the inside of its lower jaw is a curious, worm-like tongue which it wriggles like a real worm. Unsuspecting fish and even small ducklings are drawn to this lure and are instantly snapped up by the turtle's powerful hooked jaws.

Crocodiles and Alligators

What is the difference between a crocodile and an alligator?

It is easy to mistake an alligator for a crocodile, as both have armour-plated bodies and long, powerful jaws. The most obvious difference between them is in the shape of the head. Crocodiles have narrower, more pointed snouts and their lower four teeth stick out when their mouths are closed, whereas alligators' snouts are broader and more rounded.

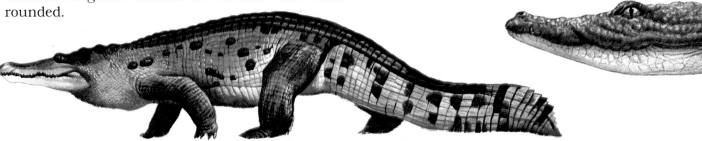

Which is the most dangerous crocodile?

The Estuarine Crocodile is the largest and most dangerous crocodile, and has been known to attack human beings. It lives mainly around coastal areas, estuaries and swamps, and is capable of swimming great distances out to sea.

Do crocodiles cry?

Crocodiles cry not because they are unhappy, but because they need to remove a lot of salt from their bodies. Crocodiles which eat a lot of salty food, such as the Estuarine Crocodile have salt-excreting glands near their eyes just for this purpose.

Why are Nile Crocodiles good parents?

Most reptiles abandon their eggs once they have laid them, but crocodiles and alligators look after them. In the case of the Nile Crocodile, both parents guard the eggs for 90 days until the young are ready to hatch. At this point the mother uncovers the eggs and both parents gently lift the hatchlings into their huge jaws. They carry the young to a special nursery area in the swamp where the parents watch over them for another three to six months until they are ready for adult life.

Crocodile

Crocodile head (above)
Alligator head (below)

Which crocodile has a head shaped like a frying pan?

The long, slim snout of the Indian Gharial sticks out from its round, flattened head rather like the handle on a frying pan. During the breeding season, the male develops a swelling on the end of his nose which is attractive to females. The long snout is particularly useful for catching fish.

The Indian Gharial

Snakes and Lizards

Rattlesnake

Are all snakes poisonous?

There are some 2700 species of snake, of which about a third are poisonous. Snake poison is known as venom, and is stored in special venom glands on the head. These venom glands are connected to hollow or grooved fangs so that when the fangs sink into a victim's skin, venom gushes through the fangs into the victim's body.

What is an egg tooth?

An egg tooth is a large, sharp tooth which baby snakes and lizards use to cut their way out through the tough, leathery eggshell. It develops on the end of the nose and soon drops off when the snake or lizard has left the egg.

Can snakes hear?

Snakes don't have ears, and so cannot hear as we do. They can, however, detect vibrations on the ground through their inner ears, and will therefore be able to feel your approaching footsteps long before you get near.

How do snakes smell?

Snakes smell both through their nostrils and with their tongues. As a snake flicks its tongue in the air it picks up scent particles. It brings them to the roof of the mouth, where a special organ 'smells' them. All snakes have this organ, which enables them to follow scent trails made by other animals.

Why do snakes shed their skins?

In fact all animals, including humans, shed their skins, due to natural wear and tear. A snake's tough skin doesn't grow as the snake gets bigger so the snake has to shed it from time to time, rather like taking off a tight coat.

How can you tell when a snake is about to shed its skin?

When a snake is about to shed its skin, or moult, its eyes go cloudy and its skin appears dull. This is because a milky fluid gathers between the old outer coat and the new skin underneath. After a few days the snake's eyes clear again and the old skin starts to peel back from the head, revealing the bright and vibrant colours of its new skin underneath. The old skin is often left behind in one whole piece, like a crumpled stocking.

A snake shedding its skin.

How do rattlesnakes rattle?

The tail of a rattlesnake is made up of hard, bell-shaped, interlocking segments. Each time the rattlesnake sheds its skin, a new segment is formed but instead of the old one dropping off with the rest of the skin, it becomes caught in the grooves of the new segment. When the snake feels threatened, its powerful muscles vibrate its tail very quickly, causing the segments to rub against each other and rattle.

How do rattlesnakes find their prey in the dark?

Rattlesnakes and other members of the Pit Viper family possess a unique method of finding prey in the dark. Located in two small pits in front of its eyes are sensitive heat detectors, capable of sensing minute rises in temperature caused by the presence of a warm-blooded animal. These heat detectors inform the snake of the distance and direction of the prey, enabling it to make an accurate strike in total darkness.

Do poisonous snakes have any enemies?

Surprisingly enough, even the most poisonous snakes have enemies. The Indian Mongoose kills cobras by biting their necks before they have a chance to strike back, while birds of prey, such as eagles and hawks, kill all snakes by tearing at them with their beaks and claws. The Common King Snake feasts on poisonous snakes after choking them to death: it seems immune to their venom and will wrestle with rattlesnakes before swallowing them head first. The poisonous snakes' worst enemies, however, are human beings who destroy the wild places where they live.

A mongoose killing a snake.

Snakes such as this Egg-eating Snake can unhinge their jaws to swallow huge pieces of food.

How do snakes manage to swallow eggs?

The neck of the Egg-eating Snake of Africa is no thicker than a human finger, yet it can swallow a hen's egg with comparative ease. Curling its body around the egg to hold it steady, it unhinges its jaws and engulfs the whole egg in a series of slow gulps. Once swallowed, the egg is broken open by a sharp-edged 'saw' at the back of its throat. The contents of the egg slide down into the snake's stomach, while the shell pieces are compressed and regurgitated.

Can snakes move in a straight line?

We normally think of snakes as creatures which wriggle along the ground in a series of S-shaped curves. Thick-bodied snakes, however, can move forwards in a perfect straight line, especially when moving in to kill. By bunching up their belly muscles, they are able to grip the ground by means of special scales on the underside of the body and advance with no sideways movement whatsoever.

Which is the longest snake in the world?

The longest snake ever to be measured was a Reticulated Python shot in Indonesia in 1912. It measured 10 metres from tip to tail. The heavier-built anacondas are thought to be able to grow even longer, although the longest one on record is nine metres long.

How do constrictor snakes kill their prey?

All pythons and boas are constrictor snakes. When hunting they grab an animal in their jaws, and then wrap the coils of their bodies around its chest. They squeeze the animal so tightly that it is unable to breathe, and so suffocates to death. The victim is then swallowed whole.

How did the Sidewinder get its name?

The Sidewinder Snake gets its name from the graceful sideways motion it adopts when crossing hot desert sands. It only touches the ground with two parts of its body at any one time and pushes itself forward in a series of sideways jumps, leaving behind a pattern in the sand like the rungs on a ladder. In this way it also reduces body contact with the hot sand and so does not overheat.

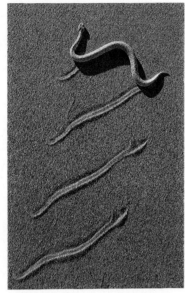

Sidewinder

How do lizards escape from predators?

A special defence mechanism used by lizards when caught by the tail is to lose it! While the predator grapples with the still-wriggling tail, the lizard makes its escape. It later grows a new tail.

How do lizards control their body temperature?

Lizards, like many other reptiles, control their body temperature by altering their behaviour. In the morning, when the lizard is cold, it will spread itself out on a sloping surface to expose as much of its body as possible to the sun. As the lizard warms up and the sun climbs higher in the sky, it turns to face the sun, so reducing the surface area exposed to heat. If the lizard becomes too hot, it raises itself up on its legs to allow free circulation of air under its belly. It may even retreat into a shady place during the hottest part of the day.

What does the Marine Iguana eat?

The Marine Iguana of the Galapagos Islands is the only living lizard to hunt for food on the sea bed, feeding almost exclusively on a diet of seaweed.

How does a chameleon catch its food?

Chameleons are highly specialized tree lizards and their ability to change colour to match their surroundings is well known. They capture their prey by means of an extremely long and sticky tongue, which is catapulted out with such speed that few insects stand a chance of escaping. On spotting a suitable prey, both eyes then work separately to give the chameleon a clearer picture of its victim. In this way the chameleon can be said to have the best all-round vision of any reptile.

Which lizard stores food in its tail?

The Gila Monster of the south-western United States is a short-legged, thick-set lizard with brightly-coloured, bead-like scales covering its body. It lives in desert areas where food is often scarce, so it has developed the ability to store fat in its tail. It lives off this fat when no other food is available. When food is plentiful the Gila Monster eats as much as possible to build up its fat stores again.

Does the Komodo Dragon breathe fire?

Unlike the fabulous winged monsters of popular myth, the Komodo Dragon does not breathe fire, nor does it fly. This solidly built animal with a huge head and long thick tail is the largest of all living lizards. It lives on a few islands in Indonesia and preys on animals such as deer and wild pigs.

The huge Komodo Dragon

BIRDS

How many birds are there?

There are about 8600 species of birds and they live in, on or above almost every part of the Earth's surface, except for the deep oceans. Different from one another in size, shape and colour, the one characteristic that unites them all is the presence of feathers – a feature which no other member of the animal kingdom possesses.

Caribbean Bee Hummingbird

Which is the smallest living bird?

The smallest bird is the Caribbean Bee Hummingbird. Weighing in at only 2 grams, it is no bigger than a large insect – indeed, some beetles weigh up to 20 times more.

Can all birds fly?

Not all birds can fly. Penguins cannot fly but use their wings as flippers for swimming underwater. Some species of cormorant, too, have lost the power of flight. Their bodies are so well adapted to swimming and diving that their wings have become too small to support their weight in flight. Some flightless land birds, such as the Australian Emu, have powerful hindlegs. These enable the birds to walk great distances and to flee from danger at considerable speed.

How do birds sleep without falling off their perches?

The group known as perching birds, or songbirds, makes up over half the number of bird species, and their feet are remarkably well adapted for grasping or perching on small twigs or stems. They always have four unwebbed toes, one of which points backwards. When they land on a perch, the weight of the body makes the leg tendons tighten, clamping the toes firmly shut.

Which is the largest living bird?

The African Ostrich, standing 2.5 metres tall and weighing up to 136 kilograms, is the largest bird alive. It is too big to fly but is the fastest creature on two legs, achieving speeds of up to 70 kilometres an hour.

The ostrich cannot fly.

Feathers

Why do birds have feathers?

There are two main reasons why birds have feathers: to keep them warm and to help them fly. Feathers may also provide birds with beautiful plumage to make them attractive to the opposite sex but this is of secondary importance to insulation and flight.

What are feathers made of?

Feathers are made of a horny protein substance called keratin. This is the same substance from which our hair and fingernails are made, the difference being in the way the feather is constructed. Keratin combines lightness with strength and flexibility, and this makes it an ideal building material for feathers.

How many feathers does a bird have?

How long is a piece of string? Birds can have any number of feathers, depending on the species; the smaller the bird, the fewer the feathers. A hummingbird's plumage may contain fewer than a thousand feathers, but a large bird such as a swan has at least 25,000. Birds tend to have more feathers in the winter than in the summer as they need more protection against the cold weather.

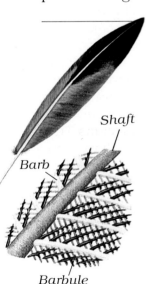

What is special about the design of a feather?

The design of a feather is special because it is so intricate. Spreading out on either side of a central hollow shaft are fine filaments called barbs, each of which is fringed by even smaller filaments called barbules. In wing feathers these barbules interlock like hooks and catches to form a continuous smooth surface over which air can flow.

Shaft

Barb

Barbule

The beautiful plumage of the Biras of Paradise is to attract members of the opposite sex.

How many different types of feather are there?

There are four main types of feather: down feathers, body feathers, wing feathers, and tail feathers. Down feathers are primarily concerned with insulation – their soft and fluffy structure enables them to trap a layer of air and so provide the bird with superb insulation. Body feathers are fluffy at the bottom and smooth at the top: only the barbules near the tip interlock, and these feathers streamline the body and increase the efficiency of flight. Wing feathers are strong and specially shaped to provide lift and manoeuvrability, while the tail feathers are used for steering, balancing and courtship.

How are birds able to fly?

Birds are able to fly because almost every part of their body is designed for flight. Their aerodynamic wings and body shape are streamlined, and their muscles and bones are specially modified. Because flying uses up huge amounts of energy, their lungs have become extremely efficient and their internal digestive system is able to release energy from food very quickly.

How do seabirds use the wind to fly?

Seabirds drift downwards on the wind until they are just above the surface of the sea, then they turn sharply to face into the wind and are lifted upwards, the wind becoming stronger the higher the bird is lifted. Once the bird has gained enough height, it turns and glides downwards again, its slender, pointed wings fully outstretched. In this way seabirds can travel great distances without exhausting all their energy.

In what ways are birds' wings adapted for flight?

Birds' wings vary in size and shape according to their different lifestyles, but generally speaking they all follow the same basic pattern. The outer part of the wing, from which the long primary feathers sprout, provides the forward push as the bird brings its wings downwards. The inner part of the wing, on which the shorter secondary feathers grow, is curved slightly from front to back to produce an aerodynamic shape that lifts the bird upwards as it moves forward. The power for flapping comes from the large chest muscles on either side of the breast bone, which are connected to the wing bones by tendons. The wings themselves contain very little muscle as they need to be light and easy to flap.

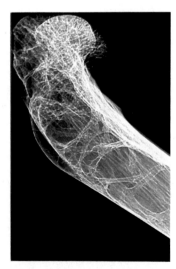

The structure of a bird bone

How do bird bones differ from those of land animals?

Bird bones are light whereas those of land animals are heavy and dense. A cross-section through a bird bone reveals that it is hollow apart from light-weight reinforcing cross struts, which help to brace the bone as the bird bends and twists through the air. Without this structure birds would be too heavy to fly.

How do birds keep flying without getting tired?

Birds use up enormous amounts of energy when they flap their wings. To reduce the amount of energy used many have evolved ways of flying, such as soaring and gliding, which don't involve flapping. When they do need to flap their wings, as during a rapid take-off, their special breathing system ensures that they are supplied with the large amounts of oxygen they need to prevent them from getting tired.

What is special about a bird's breathing system?

At first sight a bird's lungs do not look any more efficient than a mammal's. They are certainly no bigger than the lungs of a similar-sized mammal. Their secret lies in the fact that they are connected 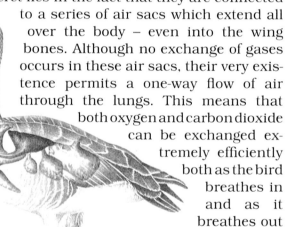 to a series of air sacs which extend all over the body – even into the wing bones. Although no exchange of gases occurs in these air sacs, their very existence permits a one-way flow of air through the lungs. This means that both oxygen and carbon dioxide can be exchanged extremely efficiently both as the bird breathes in and as it breathes out – a feat that is impossible in the 'ebb and flow' lungs of a mammal.

Inside a bird

How do birds soar?

Soaring is a form of upward gliding often used by large birds of prey to save energy. It is dependent on the warming power of the Sun. As the Sun's reflected heat warms the air at ground level, it causes the air to rise, so creating an upward thermal current. Birds such as eagles and buzzards with their long, broad wings make use of these thermals to soar to great heights, using flapping flight only to travel from one thermal to the next.

How do birds stop in mid-air without falling to the ground?

Birds stop moving forwards in the air by beating their wings non-stop; this method of flight is known as hovering. Few birds can hover for very long as it is tremendously tiring. When a kestrel hovers its tail points downwards and fans out, enabling the bird to gain lift from the passing wind. Kestrels hover mainly to look for small mammals on the ground – their keen eyes are able to spot small movements from great distances overhead.

A kestrel hovering in its search for food.

How do birds take off?

Different birds take off in different ways but most methods of lift-off involve vigorous flapping of the wings. Birds which use flight as their main means of escape from predators tend to have broad, rounded wings as these give good lift and acceleration. Many heavy land birds have to run into the wind with their wings outstretched to gain lift, while birds which spend most of their lives in the air can only take off from a high point – they literally fall into the air and then spread their wings.

Why do jays sit on ant nests?

Jays, like most other birds, suffer from tiny parasites such as lice and fleas. Snug among the bird's soft warm feathers, these unwelcome lodgers are a constant source of irritation for their host. Jays have been known to squat on an ant nest for half an hour or more in the hope that the enraged ants will swarm over their bodies and squirt poisonous formic acid at the bird's uninvited guests.

How do birds land?

Birds land by reducing their speed. They do this by swinging their bodies into an upright position, with their tail pointing down and their tail feathers spread out. The legs point forward and down to assist with braking, and many birds also briefly flap their wings backwards, as if putting themselves into reverse.

How are birds so beautifully coloured?

The colours of feathers are produced in two ways: either by pigments in the feathers, or by the way the surface of the feather scatters light. Brown and black colours come from the pigment melanin, while the brilliant blues and metallic blue-greens are caused by the way the feather reflects certain wavelengths of visible white light. White feathers are white because they reflect all the wavelengths of visible light.

The brightly coloured Quetzal

Why do birds moult?

Tough as feathers are, they wear out and become frayed with use, and have to be replaced. Most birds tend to lose only a few feathers at a time so they are always able to fly and keep warm. Some heavy-bodied waterfowl, however, would find it difficult to fly without all their flight feathers intact, so they shed and replace all their flight feathers at once. During this time they are at the mercy of predators so tend to moult in sheltered, hidden places. Birds also moult to change their plumage. Often their winter coats are thick and dull for extra warmth and camouflage, but come the breeding season the birds change their feathers for a sleeker, more brightly coloured plumage.

Why are flamingoes pink?

Flamingoes are pink because of what they eat. The red pigment called *carotenoid*, present in shrimps and other crustaceans, goes straight into the flamingo's feathers as they grow.

Flamingo

Why do birds preen themselves?

Birds preen themselves to ensure their feathers stay in good condition. Paying particular attention to its wing feathers, a bird first smears its beak with oil from a large oil gland near the base of its tail and then runs its beak through its feathers like a comb. Birds which lack oil glands, such as herons and parrots, use a fine 'powder-down' produced by special feathers.

How does a hummingbird hover?

No other bird can match the hummingbird in its ability to manoeuvre in the air. It can fly upwards, downwards, forwards, sideways – even backwards. It is able to hover motionlessly in front of a flower by beating its wings so furiously that they become all but invisible. As it hovers, it tilts its body forward, and its wings beat in a horizontal plane, providing lift but not forward movement.

Why do woodpeckers have stiff tail feathers?

Woodpeckers have stiff tail feathers to provide extra support as they peck away at the tree trunk. The tail feathers also help to brace the bird as it climbs – consequently the tips of these feathers are often worn down and ragged in appearance.

How do Barn Owls manage to fly so silently?

Barn Owls fly silently because their flight feathers are fringed. These soft fringes muffle the noise of the owls' wingbeats, allowing them to capture small animals by surprise.

Barn Owl

Eggs and Nests

Different kinds of eggs

Why do birds lay eggs?

Birds lay eggs because their reptile ancestors laid eggs, and because it has suited them to retain this characteristic. If a female gave birth to live young, or carried a developing egg around inside her body, then she would probably be unable to fly because of the extra weight. Hence birds lay their eggs as soon as possible after mating.

Why do birds build nests?

Birds build nests to protect their eggs and young from the weather and from any marauding predators. Nests also help retain the warmth of the parent bird during incubation. Bird nests vary greatly in size and shape: they can be massive structures of loose branches, or tiny cup-like containers warmly lined with hair and feathers.

A grebe nesting.

How do baby birds break out of their egg cases?

At the time of hatching, a baby chick almost fills its eggshell. Its beak is equipped with an egg tooth for chipping a hole in the shell, and at the back of its neck it has a special hatching muscle which it twitches as it pecks away at the shell. Eventually hair-line cracks develop and a tiny sliver of shell falls away, leaving a hole through which the chick can take gulps of fresh air. After a rest the chick starts chipping again around the blunt end of the egg until enough of the shell has been cracked to allow the chick to heave itself free.

Which bird sews leaves together to make its nest?

The Indian Tailor Bird makes its nest from two leaves on a large-leaved plant, piercing a series of holes on the outer edges of the leaves with its beak. It then draws the leaves together by pulling through threads of silk, grass or wool, tying each stitch separately. When a cradle shape is formed, the Tailor Bird lines it with soft fibres, and then lays two or three eggs inside.

Tailor Bird

How do mallee birds keep their eggs warm?

The mallee birds of Australia rely on the heat generated by rotting vegetation to incubate their eggs. Nest building begins with the excavation of a large pit, which the birds fill with dead leaves. They wait until after a soaking of rain, then they cover the leaves with sand, forming a smooth mound. Four months later, when the leaves have started to ferment and produce a constant temperature, the female lays the eggs inside. If it is in danger of overheating, the birds either create ventilation shafts or heap extra sand over it.

Which nests are used in birds' nest soup?

The nests of Cave Swiftlets are composed mainly of the birds' saliva, and it is these which are highly sought after as ingredients of birds' nest soup. Yet the nests are practically tasteless and of little nutritional value. Cave Swiftlets breed in huge colonies in the limestone caves of south-east Asia. They glue their nests high up on to the cave roofs.

Why does the female ostrich allow other ostriches to lay their eggs in her nest?

Female ostriches outnumber males, and so about a third of the females have no mate. The chief hen allows unattached hens to deposit their eggs in her nest as this reduces the chances of her own eggs being taken by predators. Remarkably, the chief hen is able to identify her own eggs by the pattern of pores on the white shells. She therefore makes sure that any surplus eggs which roll out of the nest are those of other females.

How big is an ostrich's egg?

An ostrich's egg is the biggest egg laid by a living bird – each one weighs up to 1.5 kilograms. Some 30 or 40 eggs are sometimes laid in a single nest, those that roll out being preyed on mostly by jackals and hyenas. Egyptian Vultures have been observed dropping stones onto the eggs from a great height, in order to break the two-millimetre thick shells.

Ostrich egg

Hen's egg

Why is the cuckoo thought to be a lazy bird?

The European cuckoo is well known for its habit of laying its eggs in the nests of other birds, notably redstarts, dunnocks and wagtails. In this way it avoids the hard work of nest-building and feeding the young, so it is easy to see how the cuckoo has earned its reputation.

What is 'dump-nesting'?

Dump-nesting is a habit practised by many birds and involves the female laying some of her eggs in the nests of other birds of the same species. Moorhens do this quite regularly and it is thought they do it as an insurance against their own nest being raided or destroyed. By not 'putting all her eggs in one basket', the moorhen increases the chances of her own offspring's survival.

What is the difference between a bird's egg and a reptile's egg?

A bird's egg has a hard, chalky shell. A reptile's egg has a more flexible, leathery outer skin. Otherwise they are very similar.

How warm do birds keep their eggs?

They keep their eggs very warm, at about 39°C (102°F). If you were that warm you would be feeling quite ill! Almost all birds keep the eggs warm by sitting on them, and many species develop brood patches on their breasts to help during incubation of the eggs. These featherless patches have a rich supply of blood vessels to make them extra warm. The Mallee Fowl, and some related species of bird, do not sit on their eggs. Instead they build mounds of rotting vegetation, like compost heaps, to keep their eggs warm. Their eggs are only kept at about 33°C (91°F).

Young cuckoo

Guillemot eggs

Why are the eggs of guillemots pear-shaped?

Guillemots do not make nests but simply lay a single egg on the bare rock of a cliff ledge. For a long time it was thought that the tapered shape of the egg had evolved as a way of stopping it rolling off the ledge: if the egg moved it rolled in a circle rather than in a straight line. Scientists now believe the main reason is that the pear shape exposes more of the egg's surface to the guillemot's warm body as it incubates the egg in a semi-standing position.

Which bird builds a communal nest?

Probably the best-known bird for communal nest-building is the Weaver Bird of south-western Africa. Each colony of birds builds a thickly-thatched, dome-like nest which provides roosting sites and nesting chambers for up to a hundred pairs of birds. This enormous nest, sometimes as much as seven metres wide, is usually built in an acacia tree. It is used by the birds all year round.

Why is the male Emperor Penguin considered to be a devoted father?

No other bird puts up with such harsh conditions as the male Emperor Penguin. Once the female has laid her single egg, she returns to the sea. The male incubates the egg on top of his feet. Huddled together on the pack ice in the darkness of an Antarctic winter, the males are unable to feed for the whole of the 64-day incubation period. When the chick hatches, the male feeds it from the secretions in his crop until the female returns to take over the care of the chick.

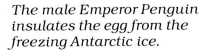

The male Emperor Penguin insulates the egg from the freezing Antarctic ice.

Which bird lays the largest egg in proportion to its size?

A fully grown New Zealand kiwi hen weighs about 1.7 kilograms (about as much as a domestic hen), and yet lays an egg which amounts to about a quarter of her own body weight. Not surprisingly, she lays only one egg at a time.

Which bird builds a false entrance to its nest?

The Cape Penduline Tit goes to extraordinary lengths to trick predators into thinking that its nest is empty. Built into its hanging nest is a false entrance leading into an 'empty' egg chamber. The real entrance to the nest is directly above the false one and has a door that can be opened and closed by the tit each time it enters or leaves the nest.

How did the Ovenbird get its name?

The common American Ovenbird is named after the domed, oven-like nest it constructs out of clay, reinforced with hair and plant material. Built on posts and bare branches, this rock-hard nest is entered by a small hole which leads to a nesting chamber about 20 centimetres wide.

Flightless Birds

Do ostriches bury their heads in the sand?

No ostrich has ever been seen doing this. The legend probably arose because of the bird's habit of laying its neck flat on the ground when sitting on its nest. This makes it less visible to its enemies; it is just like another small mound on the dry African savannah.

How does a Kiwi find food in the dark?

Kiwi The Kiwi is the national symbol of New Zealand, yet for all its fame it is a shy, nocturnal creature, seldom seen during the day. A Kiwi finds its food – typically earthworms, small insects and berries – chiefly by smell. It uses the nostrils near the tip of its long pointed beak to sniff out any tasty morsels on the forest floor.

How do penguins manage to keep warm during freezing blizzards?

Penguins are flightless birds whose feathers are devoted to keeping them warm and dry. More like dense fur than the plumage we associate with flying birds, a penguin's feathers are short and fine, and cover the birds body in a uniform thick coat. The fat stored just below the skin also provides an effective insulating layer against the cold.

Which bird is known as the South American ostrich?

The rhea, which looks very similar to the ostrich and lives in the grass- and scrublands of South America. Like the ostrich, it is a large, flightless bird capable of running swiftly. In evolutionary terms, however, rheas and ostriches are quite separate.

The huge flightless Cassowary can be very vicious. If cornered it may kick out with its powerful legs and has been known to kill people.

Why does the Cassowary bird have a helmet on its head?

The Cassowary of New Guinea is a large, solitary jungle bird. It has a powerful kick, which is sometimes used to attack unwelcome intruders. The Cassowary's bony helmet or casque is thought to protect its head as it pushes its way through the dense undergrowth; it may also be used as a tool for digging as it searches for small creatures to eat.

Beaks and Feeding

What do birds eat?

Birds have evolved to eat all sorts of food – as long as it is high in calories. Favourite foods, therefore, tend to be seeds, nuts, insects, nectar, fruit, fish and flesh. Birds prefer high-energy foods because they use up so much energy in flying.

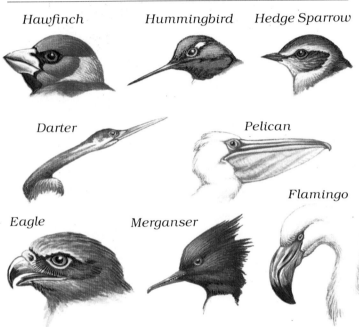

The shape of a bird's beak indicates the type of food it eats.

Why are birds' beaks all so different?

Birds' beaks are so different because they all eat different kinds of food. Seed-eaters tend to have short, strong, wedge-shaped beaks for picking and cracking seeds, while insect-eaters have thinner, pointed beaks which they use like tweezers to extract small prey. Birds which catch insects on the wing often have short beaks and wide gaping mouths which they use like fishing nets as they fly along. The beaks of flesh-eating birds are usually strong and hooked, suitable for ripping flesh off their prey.

A dissected owl pellet. Owls eat small animals whole then regurgitate the bones and skin in the form of these pellets.

What is a bird's crop?

A bird's crop is a temporary food store, located in the throat. Sometimes called a pouch or craw, this thin-walled sac enables the bird to cram more food into its beak than it can possibly hold in its stomach. At times of plenty the bird can gorge itself before retiring to a place of safety to digest its food. The crop is also a useful place to store food that will later be fed to nestlings.

Why do birds eat grit?

Seed-eating birds, such as sparrows, eat grit as an aid to digestion. The muscular part of their stomachs, known as the gizzard, has hard, ridged walls for pulverizing seeds, and this process is made even more efficient by the presence of small hard stones. Flesh- and insect-eating birds do not need to take in grit as part of their diet as their food is comparatively soft.

What are owl pellets made of?

Owl pellets consist of everying that the owl cannot digest. Unable to chew their food because they have no teeth, owls tend to swallow their prey whole – fur, feathers, bones and all. Once or twice a day owls have to regurgitate these unwanted items in the form of neat little packages called pellets. Often you can tell which species of owl made the pellet simply by examining its shape and colour. A barn owl's pellet is almost black in colour, and smooth and rounded in shape.

Swordbill Hummingbird

Why does the Swordbill Hummingbird have a beak four times the length of its body?

The beak of the Swordbill Hummingbird is long enough (10.5 centimetres) to allow it to fit neatly into the 11.4-centimetre-long flower-tube of the Andean climbing passionflower. Both flower and bird benefit from this arrangement: the flower is cross-pollinated by the bird while the bird enjoys an abundant supply of nectar.

Why do flamingoes have crooked beaks?

A flamingo's beak is crooked so that when it holds its beak upside down in the water to feed, the upper half is below the lower. As water flows in through the beak it passes over a fine sieve. This filters out any tiny animals and plant matter, before the water is pumped out again by the action of the bird's large, fleshy tongue. Baby flamingoes are not born with these complicated beaks – they rely on their parents for food until their filter-type beaks develop at about 10 weeks.

Which bird is also known as the African locust bird?

The Red-Billed Quelea is probably the most numerous bird in the world. It flies in flocks of millions and can wreak havoc on a field of cereal crops in a very short space of time. The quelea actually prefers to eat the seeds of wild grasses but when natural food supplies become exhausted, it turns to agricultural crops as a means of supplementing its diet.

Why do nightjars have bristles around their mouths?

The bristles around a nightjar's mouth are not bristles at all but fine feathers. They serve as a funnel to the bird's mouth when it is in flight. Nightjars feed mainly at night on the wing, their mouths agape to catch any winged insects in their flight path.

Do any birds have teeth?

Strictly speaking, no birds have teeth – that is, teeth that are made of bone. One group of diving ducks, however, called mergansers, has developed tooth-like serrations along the sides of their long, thin beaks. These 'teeth' are useful for gripping slippery fish underwater.

A flock of queleas

Birds of Prey

Which bird drops bones from the sky?

The Lammergeier or Bearded Vulture feeds on dead animals but when there are other vultures present at the carcass, it usually gives way to them and contents itself with a meal of bones. If the bones are too large for it to swallow, it carries them into the air and drops them from a great height, smashing them open on the rocks below. It can then get at the marrow inside.

Golden Eagle

Why do Golden Eagles only manage to rear one of their two chicks?

Golden Eagles lay two eggs but in most cases only manage to rear one chick. This is because of sibling rivalry. The first chick to hatch usually attacks its brother or sister so viciously that the younger one is forced to flee the nest. The parents do nothing to stop this aggressive behaviour.

How does the Secretary Bird kill snakes?

This long-legged African bird spends most of its time on the ground, stalking its prey on the open grassland. Occasionally it kicks or stamps furiously at a snake it has discovered in the undergrowth – even cobras and puff adders fall victim to its forceful blows. The snake is often unable to strike back because it is held at bay by the secretary bird's wings.

What do ospreys eat?

An osprey's diet consists almost entirely of fish. Ospreys catch their prey by plunging feet first into the water and then rising again with a fish grasped in both talons. The undersides of the ospreys' feet are lined with horny spines to help them grip their slippery prey.

Are Bald Eagles really bald?

These noble-looking birds, which have become the national symbol of the United States, are not really bald at all. They look bald from a distance because they have white feathers on their heads while the rest of their plumage is dark brown.

Hen Harriers

Which bird tosses food to its mate in mid-air?

The male Hen Harrier, or Marsh Hawk, catches prey for the young but does not actually return to the nest. Instead, he calls to his mate and she flies up to him, turning herself upside down in mid-air to catch the food in her talons as he drops it down to her. The female then takes the prey back to the nest to feed to the chicks.

Bald Eagles have powerful beaks for tearing flesh but often steal morsels of food from other birds.

Why are Bald Eagles sometimes known as 'pirates of the air'?

It is not unknown for Bald Eagles to rob ospreys and other smaller birds of prey of their catch by harassing them in mid-air. The smaller birds drop their prey in an act of submission, giving the eagle an easy meal. Bald Eagles are not the only birds that practise piracy in flight: certain fish eagles and Frigate Birds are also known to rob other birds of their booty.

Why are owls considered to be wise?

Owls are commonly given credit for more wisdom than they are capable of possessing. Like most birds, their behaviour is largely instinctive and their capacity for learning new tricks is limited. Their 'wisdom' probably derives from their 'human' appearance – their large heads, rounded bodies and huge forward-looking eyes are all traits with which we can identify.

Do Long-Eared Owls really have long ears?

Long-Eared Owls do have ears, but the parts that look like ears are not ears at all but long tufts of feathers. These feather tufts are in no way connected to the owl's real ears, which are tucked away at the sides of the head. In flight, the Long-Eared Owl keeps its ear tufts pressed flat against its head.

How do owls find their prey in the dark?

Owls use their keen sense of sight and hearing to locate small animals in the dark. An owl's eyes are unusually large and particularly well adapted for seeing in dim light, while its ears are superbly adapted for hearing. Situated at different levels on either side of its head, one ear picks up a sound a fraction of a second before the other, enabling the owl to pinpoint the source of the sound quite accurately. Even on the darkest nights an owl is able to home in on the scurrying movements of its prey.

Harpy Eagle

Which is the largest and most fearsome eagle in the world?

The Harpy Eagle of the South American rainforest, with its powerful legs and razor-sharp talons, is one of the world's most formidable birds of prey. Capable of manoeuvring through dense forest with great skill and agility, it gives chase to monkeys, sloths and other tree-dwelling mammals, plucking them from the branches with its huge hooked feet. Unfortunately this magnificent bird is now very rare, due to the destruction of large areas of rainforest.

Water Birds

How does the puffin keep so many fish in its beak without dropping them?

Puffins are easily recognized by their colourful striped beaks which they display to full effect during the summer breeding season. Their beaks are more than just decorative: they provide an efficient means of carrying a dozen or more small fish back to the nest to feed to their single chicks. How the puffin manages to carry such a neatly arranged row of fish in its beak without dropping them is something of a mystery. It is thought that each fish is clamped into position by special spines lining the tongue and roof of the mouth. Also, the puffin's beak is hinged in such a way as to allow fish to be gripped firmly along the whole of its length, and not just in a narrow corner.

Which bird looks as if it is walking on water?

Jacana birds don't actually walk on water – they tread on floating water plants. Their toes and claws are so extraordinarily long that their body weight is distributed over a large surface area, minimizing the danger of sinking. Jacana birds are found on ponds and in freshwater marshes throughout the Tropics.

Why do Grey Herons stand so still in the water?

Herons catch fish using stealth and surprise tactics. They stand motionless in shallow water, their necks bent, poised to stab at any fish or frog which happens to swim by. They can shoot their necks out and grasp their prey so fast that few of their victims escape.

Which birds fish together as a team?

White Pelicans are sociable birds and work together as a team to round up a shoal of fish. Once they have encircled all the fish in a particular area, they dip their beaks into the water and scoop up the fish. As the birds lift their heads the water drains out of their beaks, leaving the fish trapped inside.

Puffin

Why do avocets have upturned beaks?

The elegant upturned beaks of these black and white waders are ideally suited for sweeping the surface of mud or shallow water as the avocets pick their way along. Avocets can also swim 'up-end' like a duck. They do this when the water becomes too deep for them to stand, and sweep the bottom for their food of plant matter, insects and other small invertebrates.

How can you tell a coot's footprints from those of other waterbirds?

A coot's foot is unusual in having scaly lobes of skin growing from each of its toe bones. These scaly lobes help the bird to swim and prevent it from sinking as it walks across mud. The impression left on mud by a coot's lobed feet is instantly recognizable.

Herons are long-legged wading birds that feed on fish.

Migration

Why do birds migrate?

Birds migrate as the seasons change in order to find the food and living conditions which suit them best at different times of the year. Each year songbirds, seabirds, waterfowl and waders all make long, difficult journeys from their summer breeding quarters to their winter feeding grounds. They do this to take advantage of the seasonal variations in climate and food supply.

How do birds find their way?

Birds find their way by a variety of methods, some of which we have yet to understand. Day-flying birds are believed to use the Sun as a compass and have an in-built clock which allows them to compensate for the Sun's movements. Night-flying birds are thought to navigate by the stars. Some may use the Earth's magnetic field to guide them, and a few species are thought to be able to recognize certain geographical features, such as mountain ranges and river valleys.

Which bird flies from the North Pole to the South Pole (and back again)?

Arctic Terns must be the world's most travelled birds, spending months continuously on the wing at sea. They breed within the Arctic Circle during the summer months, and then head south for the Antarctic to take advantage of the summer season there. They cover a distance of more than 35,000 kilometres on a round trip.

Arctic Tern

Storks glide long distances during their annual migration.

Why do storks never fly over open sea?

Storks have long broad wings and combine flapping flight with soaring when flying long distances. Since soaring flight relies on thermal updraughts found only over land, storks avoid long journeys over open sea. Their migration routes over Europe and Africa cross the sea over the narrow Straits of Gibraltar or over the Bosporus at the neck of the Black Sea.

What is an irruption?

When large numbers of birds suddenly appear in an area normally considered to be outside their breeding range, we say that there has been an irruption of that particular species. Often the reason for the irruption is a shortage of food in the birds' home range – for example, seeds on which the birds normally feed may be in short supply. Birds which irrupt quite regularly include siskins, redpolls, bramblings and crossbills.

Do migrating birds always return the way they came?

Not all birds make the same outward and return journeys. The American Golden Plover, for example, leaves its arctic breeding grounds in Alaska and northern Canada and flies southwards over the Atlantic to its wintering grounds in South America. Returning adults the following spring head northwards by a different route, flying almost entirely over land via central America.

Courtship and Display

Great Crested Grebes

Are all birds faithful to their mates?

Most birds are monogamous – that is to say, they breed in pairs, and remain faithful to their mates at least until their young leave the nest. Some male birds breed with as many females as possible, and take little part in nest building or rearing the young.

Which birds build 'treasure houses'?

The male bowerbirds of Australia and New Guinea build elaborate structures, or bowers, and decorate them with colourful objects, or 'treasures' to attract females. The male Satin Bowerbird, a glossy, dark blue bird, constructs an avenue of two stick walls and decorates it with any small objects he can find – feathers, shells, flowers, even pieces of plastic – as long as they are yellow-green or preferably blue (to match his own coloration).

What is unusual about the female Red Phalarope?

The Red Phalarope is an interesting case of role reversal. Instead of the male, it is the female who takes the initiative in courting, and it is she who has the bright red plumage and chooses the nest site. After the eggs are laid, the smaller, duller male incubates them and looks after the chicks; the female goes off in search of other males.

How do male frigate birds impress females?

Frigate birds are large, fast-flying sea-birds which nest in colonies on remote tropical islands. During courtship, the male frigate bird tries to impress the female by inflating his red throat pouch to the size of a football. If the female is interested she rubs her head against his huge chest.

Why do Great Crested Grebes dance together on the water?

Great Crested Grebes perform an elegant courtship dance on the water to establish a firm pair bond. Often their display includes head shaking and taking turns to preen each other. The display ends in an exchange of weed where the two birds rise up out of the water facing each other and present their gifts.

What is a lek?

A lek is a communal display area where the breeding males of some species gather to strut and pirouette before the duller females, who watch from the edge of the lek. Birds of paradise make use of such display grounds, as do black grouse and ruffs. Typically the female selects a dominant male to mate with, and then flies away to lay her eggs and bear her own young.

Male Frigate Bird

MAMMALS

What is a mammal?

A mammal is a warm-blooded animal whose body is either wholly or partially covered in hair. Female mammals typically give birth to live young, and feed them on milk produced in special glands called *mammary glands* (from which mammals get their name). Mammals are often regarded as the most 'advanced' members of the animal world, because of their large brains and well developed senses.

How many mammals are there?

There are about 4000 species of mammal in the world, of which about half are rodents and a quarter are bats. Mammals can be divided into three groups: the *monotremes*, such as the Duck-billed Platypus and Spiny Anteater; the *marsupials*, such as the kangaroo and Koala; and the *placental* mammals, which make up most of the mammal species alive today.

What is a placenta?

Most mammals (with the exception of monotremes and marsupials) carry their young inside them where they are warm and protected. They are provided with all their nourishment through a special organ called the *placenta*. The placenta is the organ that connects mother and baby.

Placenta

What is a monotreme?

A monotreme is a mammal that lays eggs, and today only three species of monotreme are known to exist. These are the Duck-billed Platypus, and two spiny anteaters, one of which lives in Australia and the other in New Guinea. When the young hatch, they suckle milk through a modified sweat gland, not a nipple.

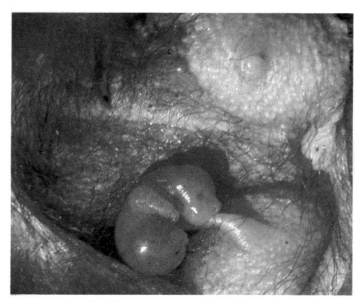

A young marsupial in its mother's pouch

When did giant mammals roam the Earth?

During the ice ages, when there were gigantic species of mammoths (elephant-like creatures), deer, buffalo, rhinoceros, sloth and armadillo. In Australia, there were giant marsupials, such as the giant kangaroo, three metres tall, and giant monotremes. Most of these very large species died out about 10,000 years ago, probably due to hunting by early man.

Why do some mammals hibernate?

Animals hibernate as a way of surviving long, cold winters. When food is scarce, an animal's best tactic is often to shut down its bodily functions and go to sleep, preferably in a sheltered, frost-free place. When hibernating, an animal's body temperature drops, its heart beat slows, and its breathing becomes shallow and infrequent. Dormice, hedgehogs, squirrels and bears all hibernate, living off the reserves of fat stored within their bodies until they stir.

What use is a tail?

Tails are bony continuations of the spine. During the course of evolution, they have come to serve different purposes for different mammals. Many use them as a means of communication – you only have to watch how a cat or dog uses its tail to learn how it communicates feelings of joy, aggression, submission and annoyance. Horses use their tails as fly whisks, while monkeys and other tree-dwellers frequently use their tails as 'fifth limbs', wrapping them around branches as they swing from tree to tree. Foxes and squirrels use their tails for balancing and stabilizing and also as warm winter coats when asleep.

Why do mammals have hair?

Mammals have hair primarily to keep them warm. But the hair on some mammals has also been modified to serve other functions. Hedgehogs have specially stiffened hair to provide them with protection, while other animals' hair may be coloured to provide an effective camouflage. Some stiffened hairs, such as cats' whiskers, are extremely sensitive to touch. Even whales, which have no body hair, have sensitive bristle-like hairs on their heads.

Hedgehogs

Why does a rat eat more than a lizard of the same size?

Because the rat is 'warm-blooded' while the lizard is 'cold-blooded'. What this means is that the rat can warm its body up by burning off some food, while the lizard cannot. So the lizard is always the same temperature as its surroundings – warm on a sunny summer's day but cold and lethargic in winter. The rat gains many advantages from being able to generate its own heat. It can keep its body at a constant, high temperature which makes it more efficient, and probably allows it to have a larger brain.

Which is the biggest mammal in the world?

The Blue Whale, which weighs up to 190 tonnes and measures some 33 metres in length. It is the largest mammal – and perhaps the largest animal – the world has ever known.

Which newborn mammals are able to look after themselves?

The young of plant-eating mammals are born in a more fully formed state than the blind, naked offspring of flesh-eating or burrow-dwelling mammals. Wildebeest, for example, are able to stand and follow their mothers within ten minutes of being born, and are able to run with the herd within 24 hours. As babies, they are extremely vulnerable to attack by predators, so the sooner they can run and hide from danger, the greater their chances of survival.

Why are scientists so interested in the Tupaia?

The Tupaia is a tree shrew found in the forests of eastern Asia. At first glance, you might wonder what makes this squirrel-like animal so interesting. The answer is that it bears a very close resemblance to the fossils of some of the earliest mammals. Scientists believe that the first mammals from which we and all other mammals descended looked and possibly behaved like the Tupaia.

Marsupials

Do all marsupials live in Australia?

Of the 250 different marsupials known, some 70 live outside the continent of Australia and its neighbouring islands. They include the opossums – the rat-like, forest-dwelling animals of North and South America. Australia has by far the greatest number and variety of marsupials, ranging from tiny marsupial mice to the large Red Kangaroos.

How are kangaroos able to survive long dry spells?

Kangaroos cope with drought in a number of ways. Firstly, they become more active at night, taking refuge from the sun under rocky outcrops and licking their arms to aid cooling by evaporation. Secondly, they are able to travel long distances to find food and water. Thirdly, their kidneys reduce water loss by excreting concentrated urine. Finally, if the female is incapable of producing enough milk, she will expel the joey from her pouch to ensure her own survival.

What is a marsupial?

A 'pouched mammal' such as a kangaroo or koala. A marsupial gives birth to its young when they are very small, like tiny pink worms. The young climb through the mother's fur into a pouch where they feed on milk until they are large enough to leave. Although most marsupials live in Australia, some are found in New Guinea and the Americas.

Do kangaroos live in trees?

Three species of kangaroo have taken to a life in the trees. These tree kangaroos are remarkably agile, and can take flying leaps from tree to tree, using their long tails to help them balance. Their front feet have long curved claws for gripping branches. Unlike many other tree-dwelling animals, they have still retained the ability to hop rapidly along the ground, and frequently come down from the trees to graze.

Marsupials, such as the kangaroo, carry their young in a pouch until they start to fend for themselves.

Why do kangaroos hop?

Nobody knows precisely why kangaroos hop instead of running on all fours. In terms of energy use, hopping is thought to be a more efficient way of getting about at speeds of over 12 kilometres per hour. Their babies are also less likely to fall out of the pouch if the kangaroo maintains a more upright position while hopping along.

What is so unusual about the Duck-billed Platypus?

Few mammals are as strange as the Duck-billed Platypus. Not only is it a monotreme (an egg-laying mammal), it also has webbed feet and a duck-like bill. These strange adaptations make this furry mammal perfectly adapted to its waterside life. Probing the muddy river bottom with its sensitive beak, it eagerly feeds on prawns, worms and larvae and sometimes consumes as much as one kilogram of food each day. It lives in a system of burrows in the river bank, which it excavates using its sharp claws.

The Duck-billed Platypus is a mammal that lays eggs.

What do Numbats eat?

Numbats are the marsupial equivalent of anteaters: they have long snouts, long sticky tongues and strong claws for digging termites out of their nests. Once called Banded Anteaters because of their stripey coats, these rat-sized creatures may consume up to 20,000 termites a day.

How small is a baby kangaroo when it is born?

The Red Kangaroo is the biggest of all the marsupial mammals. It can weigh up to 70 kilograms, yet its baby (or 'joey') weighs less than a gram at birth. Despite being so tiny, the joey has well-formed front claws with which it is able to clamber up its mother's belly and into her pouch. Once fastened to a nipple, the joey continues its development in the pouch for eight months, before venturing out on its own.

Why is the koala considered to be a fussy eater?

The koala is very selective in what it eats – only the leaves and shoots of 12 species of eucalyptus tree will do. The female carries her baby about on her back for six months after it has left the pouch, feeding it on a diet of semi-digested leaves.

Koalas

Wombats are Australian burrowing marsupials.

Where do wombats live?

Wombats live underground in a series of long inter-connecting burrows, which are dug with their powerful front claws. Often compared with the European Badger, these strongly built marsupials exist on a diet of plant roots, tubers and grass. Wombats are sometimes kept as pets, because they are quite docile and easy to feed.

What is a Potoroo?

A Potoroo is a small, rat-like kangaroo which lives in the forests and woods of Tasmania and eastern Australia. It is active mainly at night, and hops around just like its larger relatives, feeding on plant roots, tubers and insects.

Which mammal dies after mating?

The Swamp or Brown Antechinus is a tiny mouse-sized creature which is common among the soil and leaf litter of the forests of eastern Australia. The male only mates once in his short life, after which he dies, whereas the female will sometimes go on to produce a second litter.

Do all female marsupials have pouches?

Not all marsupials have sophisticated pouches for carrying their young. Many mouse-sized marsupials of the family Dasyuridae simply carry their young underneath them like bunches of grapes with the young firmly fastened to their mother's nipples. When the young become too heavy to carry, the mother deposits them in a specially prepared nest.

How did the Tasmanian Devil get its name?

The first settlers to Australia believed this stocky marsupial to be a savage and ruthless killer of sheep, and named it accordingly. The Tasmanian Devil though, is more of a scavenger than a hunter. Its large head and strong jaws enable it to crunch through the bones of dead animals with comparative ease.

Tasmanian Devil

What do you do if you 'play possum'?

To 'play possum' is to pretend to be dead. The Common American Opossum gave rise to this expression because of the dramatic way it pretends to be dead when threatened by a predator. Its eyes close, its mouth falls open, its breathing virtually stops and its body becomes paralysed. Many attackers lose interest if they think their intended victim is dead, as some predators only kill live prey.

The Insect-eaters

What is a rodent?

Rodents are the commonest group of mammals alive in the world, and include rats, mice, voles, squirrels, beavers and porcupines. They are small- to medium-sized animals with chisel-shaped front teeth which are good for gnawing. Their success in populating the Earth's land surface must partly be due to their fast breeding rate.

A rabbit with its young

How many mice can a single breeding pair give rise to in a year?

At six weeks old a female mouse can start to breed, producing around five to seven babies in a litter. If a single breeding pair has ten litters in a year, and if all their young survive and reproduce, then that one pair will have given rise to half a million mice in just one year.

Which is the largest rodent in the world?

The largest rodent in the world is the South American Capybara. It measures over one metre from its muzzle to the base of its stumpy tail and has been likened to a small hippopotamus, when viewed from a distance. Capybaras are excellent swimmers and live in small groups near fresh water.

Porcupines release a powerful cloying scent when threatened.

How does the porcupine behave when threatened?

A threatened porcupine will rattle its quills and give off a powerful smell in an attempt to deter its attacker. If it continues to be threatened, however, it will charge backwards into its enemy, ramming its sharp, backward-curving quills into its body. The spines come away easily, and can cause permanent damage to a predator, if not removed.

Which rodent has no fur?

The Naked Mole-rat is a most peculiar mammal. Not only does it lack any fur, but it also lives in a colony governed by a single breeding queen. It spends its whole life underground in a large tunnel system (which extends for up to three kilometres), with 'worker' mole rats gathering roots and tubers for the whole colony to eat. So well insulated is the colony from changes in the outside temperature, that the Naked Mole-Rat has no need for thick fur.

How fast do the teeth of a pocket gopher grow?

The pocket gopher is a North American rodent which lives in underground burrows. Its front teeth, like those of other rodents, never stop growing and increase by up to 40 centimetres a year. Because its teeth are being constantly worn down by gnawing and chewing they remain the same length.

Why do rabbits wash behind their ears?

A rabbit washes its ears by repeatedly licking its forepaws and running them over the surface of its ears. It does this not just to keep its ears clean, but also to take into its mouth the natural oil which covers the ear surface. This oil is important in forming vitamin D – which in turn is necessary for healthy bone growth. If the rabbit is prevented from doing this, it will develop rickets.

Do lemmings commit suicide?

Lemmings are small, stout animals with short tails and small eyes, which live in the mountains of Scandinavia. Every three or four years their numbers increase dramatically, causing mass migration of thousands of lemmings down from the mountains in search of food. Contrary to popular belief they do not rush headlong to their deaths when they reach the sea, but their journey is dangerous and many of them die when crossing rivers and roads, and many are eaten by predators.

A beaver felling a tree.

Why do beavers build dams?

Beavers build dams to create their own ponds. That way they can keep the level of the water artificially deep for the construction of their house or 'lodge'. The lodge is a dome-shaped pile of sticks and mud surrounded by water and contains three or four rooms, each with underwater entrances. These entrances have to be well below the surface so they do not freeze during the winter. No other wild animal has such a dramatic effect on the landscape as the beaver. Their dams can cause flooding for miles around, killing trees and plants and creating new wetlands.

Why are you more likely to see a Grey Squirrel than a Red Squirrel in Britain?

Grey Squirrels from North America were introduced into Britain at the beginning of the 20th century. Until then the only squirrels to be seen were red ones. Since then, the numbers of Red Squirrel have declined, as the natural pine forests in which they live have been felled and cleared. The Grey Squirrels, on the other hand, are more adaptable than the Red, and this may account for the rapid increase in their numbers.

A section through a system of burrows dug by lemmings.

How do bats fly?

Bats are the only mammals whose front limbs have been specially modified for powered flight (as opposed to gliding). Stretching from the neck to the wrist, across elongated fingers and finally to the ankle (and sometimes the tail), is a thin sheet of skin which forms the bat's wings. These wings have an aerodynamic shape when extended. Although bats are good fliers once airborne, few are capable of lifting themselves into the air from the ground. Free-tailed bats allow themselves to drop a couple of metres from the ceilings of their cave roosts before taking flight. Vampire Bats jump high into the air to become airborne.

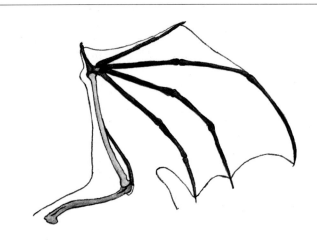

Bat's wings have similar structures to our hands. The five dark areas are equivalent to fingers, the forearm and upper arm are also visible.

How do bats find their way in the dark?

Bats use sound to find their way in the dark. They send out high-pitched squeaks then listen for the echoes as the sounds bounce off objects in their path. The bat is able to build up a 'sound picture' in its brain based on the pattern of incoming echoes – and can even locate tiny insects accurately.

Which bat feeds her milk to the offspring of other bats?

The Mexican Free-tailed Bat congregates in enormous numbers in caves in Texas and New Mexico – some colonies may consist of more than ten million bats! At night the females leave the young in the safety of the roost. On their return, the females do not seek out their own offspring, but feed the first young bats they find.

Which mammal has a diet of pure blood?

The Vampire Bat of tropical America lives on the blood of other animals and spends about half an hour each night feeding. Vampire Bats do not actually suck the blood through the puncture wounds made by their fangs: they lap it up from the small incision made by their razor-like front teeth. Their saliva contains an anti-clotting agent, and the blood simply oozes out while the victim continues to sleep. Although the amount of blood lost by the victim is usually small, there is a risk that the bat can transmit diseases, such as rabies, to its host.

Why does the Bulldog Bat of Mexico have such long legs?

In addition to its diet of insects, the Bulldog Bat also eats fish. To catch them, it flies low over the water, using its echo-location system to detect any ripples or disturbances in the water. Occasionally it will dip its large clawed feet into the water and 'trawl' the surface for fish. If it catches one, the bat swings the fish up to its mouth and flies on, chewing its catch in mid-air.

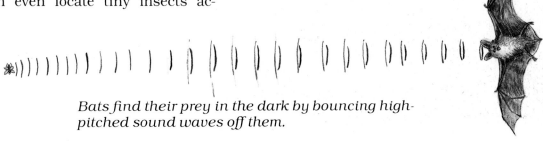

Bats find their prey in the dark by bouncing high-pitched sound waves off them.

What is an insectivore?

An insectivore is an animal that eats insects and other small invertebrates. Hedgehogs, tenrecs, golden moles, moonrats and shrews are all insectivores.

How does the Moonrat repel its enemies?

The south-east Asian Moonrat is an unkempt-looking creature with a whitish head, a black body and a long scaly tail. When excited or threatened, it releases an unpleasant odour of rotten onions, which is often strong enough to deter all but the most persistent predators.

Which mammal has a poisonous bite?

The Short-tailed Shrew of North America is the only mammal known to have poison glands in its mouth. The poison is secreted into its saliva and when the shrew bites its prey, the poison seeps into the victim's blood. Mice and other small animals are quickly paralysed – even humans can suffer a painful wound if bitten by this shrew.

How are moles adapted to a life underground?

Most moles live underground. To do this they have a pair of spade-like claws on their front feet for digging burrows. They move backwards and forwards with equal ease and they have sensitive bristles on their noses and tails which help them find their way. A mole's eyes tend to be small as they are of little use underground, and their fur is short and dense, so as not to become matted with earth.

Anteater

Why does the Giant Anteater walk on its knuckles?

The Giant Anteater walks on its knuckles to protect the long sharp claws on its front limbs. It uses these powerful claws to rip open ant or termite mounds, feeding on the vast quantities of insects inside. The Giant Anteater's tongue is coated in a sticky saliva, allowing it to pick up large numbers of ants at a time.

What is a pangolin?

The African Pangolin is a very unusual-looking anteater. Like other anteaters, it has a long nose with an even longer sticky tongue, and its body is covered with enormous, overlapping horny scales, so that it looks like a huge pine cone! It uses its long tail for gripping (in the case of the Tree Pangolin) and balancing, and has very strong front claws to demolish the nests of ants and termites.

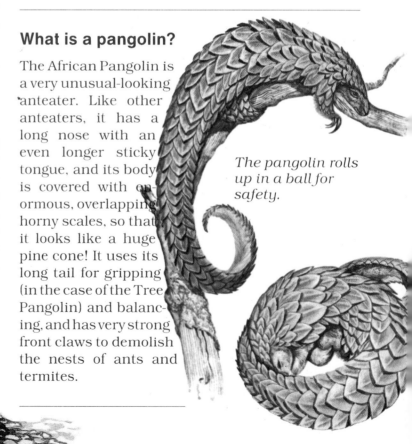

The pangolin rolls up in a ball for safety.

The burrowing mole

Marine Mammals

What do whales eat?

There are two sorts of whale: toothed whales and baleen whales. Toothed whales tend to be much smaller than baleen whales, and they feed on fish and squid. They include the dolphins, porpoises and small whales. Baleen whales are the true giants of the ocean. They have no teeth, but have triangular plates of horny material known as baleen, which act as giant strainers. Baleen whales feed on tiny shrimp-like animals called krill, which they filter out of the water through their sieve-like baleen plates.

Whales breathe through a hole in their head. Underwater this remains tightly closed.

Why do whales grow so large?

These gentle creatures spend their lives peacefully cruising along through the water filtering their food, so have no need to reduce their size to acquire speed and agility. Unlike land animals, whose bones could not support such a huge weight, the whale's body is supported by water, so there is no theoretical limit to its size. Also, there are positive advantages to being large. Firstly, it is easier for a large animal to keep warm than a small one, because of the smaller surface area to volume ratio. Secondly, the sheer bulk of these animals is enough to deter most ocean-going predators.

How often do whales need to breathe air?

Whales need to breathe air much less frequently than land-living mammals because they can store oxygen in their muscles. They also clear the used air from their lungs much more efficiently than humans can. When they rise to the surface, 90 per cent of the spent air in their lungs is blown out through the blowhole on the top of the head. In this way more oxygen is taken in and the whales can stay underwater for up to two hours without drawing breath.

How do whales keep warm in icy waters?

Whales rely on a thick insulating layer of blubber to keep their bodies warm in cold water. This blubber is not soft and rubbery, but hard and compact – in some species as thick as 50 centimetres.

Why is a dead whale sometimes called a burnt whale?

The layer of blubber is so efficient at retaining heat that a dead whale may literally start to cook as decomposition sets in and raises the internal temperature. Normally a living whale will control heat build-up inside its body during bursts of activity by increasing the flow of blood to the surface of the skin.

Humpback Whale

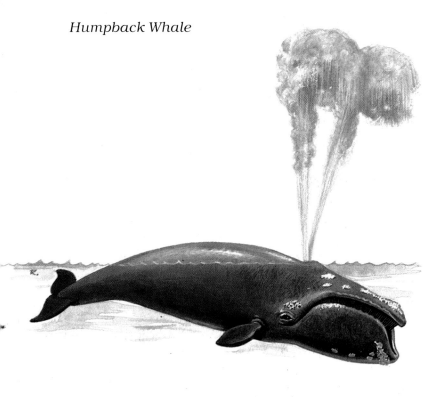

Why do Humpback Whales sing?

Humpback Whales are the most musical of all the mammals, and their songs are extraordinarily complex, lasting up to half an hour. No-one knows the real reason why the Humpback Whale sings: it could be a means of letting other whales know their whereabouts and to identify the individual making the song. Sound travels much more efficiently in water than in air and the songs of the Humpback Whales may be heard for hundreds of kilometres.

What do dolphins have in common with bats?

Both bats and dolphins use echo-location or sonar to find their prey. They give out a series of extremely fast clicks in different frequencies and by analysing the quality of the echoes, dolphins are able to 'see' clearly in dark water. It is thought that their bulging foreheads, which house a pad of tissue called the *melon*, may help to focus the sound beams.

What do Killer Whales kill?

Killer Whales are not fussy eaters – they will kill fish, squid, sea lions, seals, birds and even dolphins and porpoises. They commonly hunt in packs, and will fearlessly attack whales bigger than themselves. They are very fast swimmers, and can travel at speeds of more than ten kilometres per hour for considerable distances.

What is a Dugong?

A Dugong is sometimes called a sea-cow, after its habit of grazing on marine grasses on the sea bed. Except for whales, it is the only mammal to spend its whole life at sea, growing up to three metres in length. Dugongs can be found mainly in the coastal waters of the Indian Ocean and around Australia, although their numbers have declined due to over-hunting.

Dugong

What is the difference between a sea lion and a seal?

Sea lions and seals can most readily be distinguished on land by looking at their flippers and hind limbs. A sea lion can turn its hind limbs forward and use its front flippers as 'props' when on land, allowing it to waddle about. A seal's limbs, however, are too short to be of any use on land, and consequently it 'humps' its body along. Sea lions also have external ears whereas seals do not.

A walrus, showing its large tusks.

What colour are white whales when they are born?

The usual colour of white whales or belugas is to help camouflage them against Arctic the pack ice. At birth the young are dark brownish-red, turning blue-grey as they get older. It is not until they reach maturity at six years that their skins have paled to a creamy yellow colour.

Why do walruses have tusks?

Walruses use their tusks as ice picks when clambering over ice and rocks. Male walruses also use them as weapons to fight off predators and other male walruses during the breeding season. In addition it is thought that the tusks serve as useful dredges as the walrus rakes the sea bed for molluscs and small crustaceans.

Why is seal milk so rich and creamy?

Seal milk is very rich in fat so that seal pups put on weight as quickly as possible. Seals come on to land to give birth and nurse their young at which time the pups are very vulnerable to attack by predators, and it is in their interests to cut down the period that they spend out of the water. The provision of a creamy milk is one way of doing this.

Do all seals live in the sea?

Not all seals live in the sea – there is one species of seal which lives only in fresh water, and that is the Baikal Seal of Lake Baikal in Siberia. Lake Baikal is probably the deepest lake in the world, and the Baikal Seal spends most of its life in the northernmost part.

How big is an Elephant Seal?

The Elephant Seal is the biggest seal in the world, growing to a length of six metres and weighing as much as three tonnes. Its name comes not only from its size, but from the elephant-like trunk which protrudes from the male's head.

Elephant Seal

Hoofed Herbivores

Pigs, sheep and cattle are all ungulates.

What is an ungulate?

An ungulate is a hoofed, plant-eating mammal, whose feet are usually well adapted for running on open ground. Ungulates tend to live in herds, and can be divided into two main groups: odd-toed and even-toed mammals. The odd-toed mammals have one or three toes on each foot, and include horses, tapirs and rhinoceroses. The even-toed mammals usually have two or four toes, and include antelopes, camels and pigs.

Why do some animals 'chew the cud'?

Animals which 'chew the cud' are called *ruminants*, and they do this as a means of digesting fibrous plant material. The stomach of a ruminant is a complex, four-chambered organ, and freshly-eaten food is passed straight into the first chamber, or *rumen*. Here it is exposed to the action of bacteria and digestive enzymes for several hours, before being returned to the mouth as *cud* for a thorough chewing. The chewed cud is then swallowed into the stomach proper, where it can finally be absorbed into the animal's bloodstream. Animals which chew the cud are all even-toed, and include antelope, deer, giraffe and sheep.

Why do antelopes graze in large herds?

The open plains where antelopes graze provide little protection from predators, and so antelopes (as well as many other grazing mammals) seek safety in large numbers. With so many pairs of eyes, ears and nostrils constantly on the alert, it is virtually impossible for a predator to spring a surprise attack. Also, large numbers of animals fleeing in all directions can confuse a predator, giving the prey a better chance of escape.

What is the difference between horns and antlers?

The main difference between horns and antlers is that horns are permanent, whereas antlers are not. All members of the deer family (except the Chinese Water Deer) possess antlers, which are shed each year at the end of the breeding season. Antlers are long, branching structures made of bone, while horns tend to have a bony core covered in hard skin-tissue.

The antlers on Red Deer are covered in soft skin.

What are horns and antlers used for?

Contrary to what many people think, the chief use of horns and antlers is not to fight off predators, although they are used occasionally for this purpose. Their main function is to establish sexual dominance within herds. During the breeding season, males of the same species may often be seen locked in combat, their horns or antlers intertwined, as they battle for the right to breed with the females.

The Indian Elephant (top) *and African Elephant* (above) *are easily distinguished by the head shape. The African Elephant has much larger ears and a more rounded head.*

What is the difference between an African and an Indian elephant?

The most obvious difference is in the size of the ears: African elephants have larger ears, which help them to keep cool in the hot African climate. The Indian elephant may also be recognized by its more humped back and shorter tusks. Both elephants have been persecuted for their ivory tusks, and although hunting is now controlled, poaching still continues to this day.

Are warthogs really warty?

Warthogs are members of the pig family which, in addition to grazing grass, rummage about on the African savannah in search of roots, tubers, berries and even small mammals. Their large heads bear four upward-curving tusks and four warty growths (two on each side), from which the animal derives its name.

How can you tell a reindeer from a caribou?

Visually, you cannot tell a reindeer and a caribou apart because they are effectively the same species. They both vary in colour from dark brown to almost white and they congregate in vast herds on the arctic tundra. Reindeer and caribou are distinguished only by their range: reindeer live in northern Europe and Asia, while caribou are found in North America.

Which antelope walks on tip-toe?

The literal translation of the African Klipspringer's name is 'rock jumper', which seems appropriate as it is the only hoofed mammal south of the Sahara to leap about on rocky mountain ridges with ease and agility. The fact that it walks on the tip rather than the flat of its hoofs allows it to climb almost vertical rock faces.

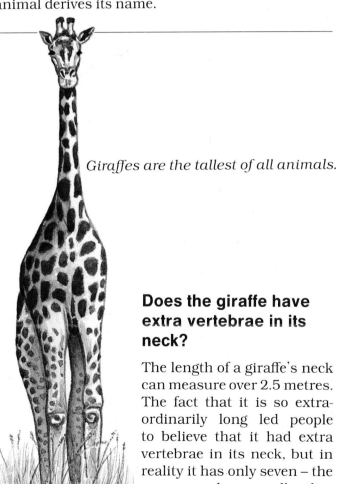

Giraffes are the tallest of all animals.

Does the giraffe have extra vertebrae in its neck?

The length of a giraffe's neck can measure over 2.5 metres. The fact that it is so extraordinarily long led people to believe that it had extra vertebrae in its neck, but in reality it has only seven – the same number as all other mammals.

Which animal is the closest relative to the elephant?

Unbelievable as it may seem, the tiny rodent-like Rock Hyrax is the elephant's closest relative. This stocky little African animal, with short ears and no tail to speak of, is the only hoofed mammal properly able to climb trees. The tops of its feet have flattened nails rather than claws, which give a hoof-like appearance, while the bottoms have soft suction pads, which help the hyrax to climb.

Do camels store water in their humps?

Camels do not store water but fat in their humps. The fat can be broken down when food and water are scarce, to provide energy and water. Camels are uniquely adapted to a life in the desert: because all their fat is stored in their humps, the rest of their body-surface is free to get rid of excess heat. Their feet, too, are specially adapted to walking across the desert with two large toes on each foot providing a large surface area to prevent the camel from sinking in the sand.

Why do hippopotamuses yawn?

Hippopotamuses yawn not because they are tired but to issue a warning to other hippopotamuses. Male hippopotamuses can be very aggressive during the breeding season, and when they yawn they reveal huge teeth which are capable of inflicting severe wounds. Hippopotamuses spend much of the day submerged in water, with just their eyes, ears and nostrils above the surface. At dusk they emerge to feed on the riverside grasses and plants.

Hippopotamuses spend most of the day under water.

Are White Rhinoceroses paler than Black Rhinoceroses?

White Rhinoceroses are in fact no paler than Black Rhinoceroses – the name probably arose from an Afrikaans word for *wide*, referring to the rhinoceros' broad mouth. White Rhinoceroses are the second-largest living land animals after the elephant, and they are generally placid, grass-eating creatures, despite their fierce appearance. Black Rhinoceroses tend to be smaller and less sociable, and feed on leaves and shoots.

Camels, the 'ships of the desert'.

Which is the largest living deer?

The Moose or Elk of northern Canada and northern Europe and Asia is the largest deer, at over three metres tall. Its antlers are broad and flattened, and a flap of skin known as the *bell* hangs from its throat. Outside the breeding season, they are solitary animals, and frequently wade into rivers and lakes to feed on the water plants.

The Flesh-eaters

How do lions hunt their prey?

Lions are the only cats which live and hunt together in groups, called *prides*. Usually it is the lionesses who do the hunting, as they are sleeker and more agile than the males, who have heavier bodies and shaggy manes. Often several lionesses will stalk and encircle a group of prey (antelope, gazelle or wildebeest), drawing as close as possible before attacking. Lionesses kill by giving a swift bite to the neck or throat. After the kill has been made, the males will push their way through the lionesses to demand their share.

Lions and (above right) *lionesses.*

Which is the fastest of all living hunters?

The streamlined cheetah, with its long legs and supple body, is the fastest mammal on Earth, achieving speeds of over 100 kilometres per hour. It can only run fast in short bursts, lacking the stamina for a prolonged chase. Its main prey are hares, small antelope and birds.

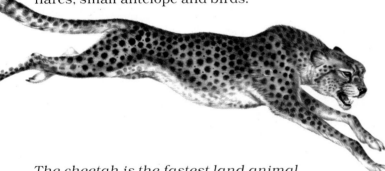

The cheetah is the fastest land animal.

Why are hyenas such successful hunters?

The hyenas are the most successful hunters of the African savannah not because of their speed – they rarely run faster than 65 kilometres per hour – but because of their co-operative team spirit. Hyenas hunt at night in packs and communicate using a rich vocabulary of howling screams and whooping laughs. They are capable of bringing down animals much larger than themselves, such as zebras and antelopes, and they pursue their prey doggedly until it finally succumbs. The pack devours every part of the carcass except for the skull.

Why does the Fennec Fox have such large ears?

The Fennec Fox of the Sahara is the smallest of all the foxes, and yet, proportionally to the size of its body, it has the largest ears of all the carnivores. It has large ears for two reasons: firstly, to help it pinpoint the smallest sound made by any potential prey moving around in the dark; and secondly, to get rid of any excess heat.

Are domestic dogs related to wolves?

Yes. Most scientists now believe that every breed of dog known today is descended from one wild species, the common wolf of Europe and Asia. It is possible that other wild species, such as jackals, have played a part in the origin of modern dogs, but this is unlikely. The oldest fossil remains of dogs have been found in Europe and the Middle East and are about 9,000–11,000 years old. Dogs were probably domesticated long before that.

Why does the tiger have a stripey coat?

The tiger is the largest of the big cats, and usually hunts alone at dusk. Its coat is striped to enable it to blend in with the background vegetation as it stalks its prey – usually deer, wild cattle or pigs. Often a tiger will pounce on its victim as it pauses to drink at a waterhole, killing it by squeezing its throat.

A well-camouflaged tiger

Why do Meerkats constantly look up at the sky?

Meerkats are sharp-nosed mongooses with greyish-brown fur which is banded across the back. They live in small communities in the South African bush country, and their homes consist of a series of underground burrows. They spend large parts of their day sitting on their haunches gazing skywards, constantly on the look-out for hawks and eagles. Should one pass overhead, an alarm goes up, and the whole colony will freeze, watching the bird intently. At any sign of attack, they dive headlong into their burrows.

What is the difference between a puma, mountain lion and a cougar?

Technically there is no difference. All names are given to the animal generally known as the puma. This large feline looks something like a lioness, with short yellowish-brown fur and has similar dimensions. It is found from Western Canada to the southern half of South America. The puma is a very athletic animal and can cover up to 6 metres in one leap.

Puma

How smelly is a skunk?

Skunks themselves aren't smelly, but the liquid they eject from their stink glands is so repulsive that it can temporarily stop its victim from breathing. So confident are skunks of their defensive weaponry, that they wander about at dusk in search of their prey (insects, small animals and berries) in a leisurely, almost brazen manner. Their bold black and white markings serve as a warning to potential predators, and they will erect their tails in a threatening posture if they sense danger.

Why do leopards hang their prey in trees?

Leopards are opportunistic hunters – they will kill all sorts of creatures, including monkeys, snakes and domestic cattle. Large prey, such as gazelles and antelopes, are frequently dragged up into trees and hung over the branches in order to avoid the attentions of other flesh-eaters. Even vultures find it difficult to rob a leopard of its catch if it is wedged in a tree.

Why do dogs bury bones?

In the wild, dogs and foxes have a natural tendency to store any leftover food. A Red Fox which has killed more food than it can eat will dig a hole and bury the surplus, returning to it later when it is hungry. The domestic dog's habit of burying bones is simply a natural urge that it has retained from its wild ancestors.

Which is the greediest of all the carnivores?

The wolverine of Scandinavia and North America has earned this dubious reputation, frequently attacking animals much larger than itself. It is immensely strong and has a huge appetite.

The wolverine often kills animals that it does not even want to eat.

Why do aardwolves look like striped hyenas?

Both the aardwolf and the striped hyena have sloping backs, pointed ears and a mane composed of stiff hairs along their backs which, when erected, make them look bigger than they really are. But whereas the hyena is equipped with sharp teeth and powerful jaws, the aardwolf has a comparatively weak mouth and small teeth, being adapted for eating termites. The aardwolf has good reasons for mimicking the hyena, for it is less likely to be attacked by large predators such as leopards if the predator mistakes it for a more vicious opponent.

How does the Honey Badger find honey?

The Honey Badger, or Ratel, of Africa and southern Asia is a stocky animal with an extremely tough skin which protects it from bee stings. It is very partial to honey, and has developed a very special relationship with a small bird called the Black-throated Honeyguide. When the honeyguide finds a bees' nest, it gives a characteristic call, which attracts the attention of any Ratels in the area. The Ratel will follow the bird to the nest and break it open with its powerful foreclaws, and both partners will then feast on the spoils.

Are all Brown Bears brown?

Big brown bears, such as the Grizzly are not always brown, but can be any colour ranging from yellowish fawn to nearly black. They are large, powerfully built bears which enjoy a varied diet of insects, plants, fish and small mammals. In the autumn the bears fatten up on fruit and berries in preparation for their winter sleep.

Why do cats have rough tongues?

A cat's tongue is rough so that it can rasp small pieces of meat off bones or lick the hairs off the skins of dead animals. A rough tongue is also a useful grooming aid, which the cat puts to regular use when cleaning its fur.

The Brown Bear

Primates

Three different types of monkey, the Proboscis (above left), *the Woolly monkey* (above centre) *and the Red Colobus*

What is a primate?

A primate is considered to be the most highly developed of all mammals: it has a large brain, keen senses of hearing, touch and vision, and a generalized skeleton, with five digits on the end of each of its limbs.

How many different kinds of primate are there?

There are 179 species of primate, and these fall into two groups: the prosimians, or primitive primates, which include the lemurs, aye-ayes and bushbabies; and the higher primates, which include monkeys, apes and humans.

What is the difference between monkeys and apes?

The main difference between monkeys and apes is that apes – orang-utans, gorillas, chimpanzees and gibbons – have no tails. Both apes and monkeys walk on all fours, but apes adopt a more upright position.

How are monkeys suited to a life in the trees?

Monkeys are adapted to their tree-top lifestyle because they have a pair of forward-facing eyes (enabling them to judge distances) and long arms with grasping hands. Monkeys are therefore able to move about easily in the trees without having to descend. They move quickly and fluently through the tree tops swinging from branch to branch, or climbing between trees directly in the dense forest canopy.

What is the fastest-moving monkey in the world?

The Patas Monkey, found on the dry savannahs of central Africa. Because trees are few and far between in these grasslands, Patas Monkeys have to run fast to escape danger – they cannot leap into the nearest tree as can most monkeys. The Patas Monkey can run at up to 55 kilometres per hour over short distances.

How intelligent are apes?

Apes are highly intelligent animals: in the wild they use sticks as tools for extracting termites from their nests, and in captivity they learn tricks very easily. Some chimpanzees have even been taught how to communicate in sign language.

Gorilla

Are gorillas fierce animals?

Few animals have been as maligned as the gorilla. For despite its large and robust appearance, it is a quiet, peaceful animal with few real enemies (apart from human beings). Gorillas live in small family groups in the rainforests of central Africa. Their diet consists of leaves, stalks, berries and nettles, which are always in plentiful supply. If a male gorilla feels threatened or annoyed, he will stand up and beat his chest – and may even charge at the intruder – but much of this behaviour is bluff and rarely comes to blows.

Which monkeys prefer to live on the ground?

Baboons spend most of their waking time on the ground, searching for food in troops of 20–200 animals, depending on the species. Most baboons are omnivorous, enjoying a mixed diet of fruit, seeds, leaves, roots, insects and small mammals. At night they seek the safety of the trees for sleeping.

Baboons spend most of their time on the ground.

Where do chimpanzees sleep at night?

Chimpanzees seek the safety of the trees at night, and every evening each chimpanzee builds its own sleeping nest. They usually choose a secure place in the crown of the tree or in the fork of a stout branch to make their beds, bending over leafy twigs to make a springy mattress. The whole operation takes about five minutes. A female who has just given birth generally takes longer to build a larger, more substantial nest.

What does the Ring-tailed Lemur use its tail for?

The Ring-tailed Lemurs of Madagascar have beautifully banded, black and white tails which they hold aloft like banners as they walk on all fours across the ground. Because much of their time is spent in troops, their tails provide a useful means of communication with one another. The males also use their tails to threaten each other: contesting males smear their tails with scent from glands on their upper arms and then brandish them over their backs, wafting the scent forward in an aggressive manner.

WHERE ANIMALS LIVE

The Polar Regions

How many penguins does a Polar Bear catch in a year?

None! Polar Bears only live around the Arctic. Penguins only live around the Antarctic. So they never meet.

How big is the smallest land animal in the Antarctic?

Only 12 millimetres long. It is a flightless midge. There are very few land animals in Antarctica because there are so few plants, and the temperatures are so low. Most of the animals found on land are tiny invertebrates, too small to be seen without a microscope. There are only 112 species of arthropod, whereas most continents have millions.

Where does an Emperor Penguin spend the winter?

Female Emperor Penguins spend the winter at sea, feeding. But male Emperor Penguins spend the worst two months of the winter standing on the Antarctic ice. The temperature averages $-20°C$ and the winds can blow at up to 200 kilometres per hour. It is constantly dark and there is no food.

Why are Adelie Penguins reluctant to enter the water?

Individual Adelie Penguins often hesitate at the water's edge for fear of being caught by the voracious Leopard Seal. This streamlined hunter of the Southern Ocean is particularly adept at snapping up penguins as they move off the ice.

Why don't polar animals freeze solid when temperatures fall below freezing?

They have chemicals in their body that act as 'anti-freeze', rather like the anti-freeze that stops the water in car radiators from turning to ice in the winter. The main anti-freeze chemical in living things is *glycerol*. It stops the water from forming ice crystals, so it cannot freeze, even though the temperature is lower than in a deep-freeze. A whole range of animals from fish to insects have anti-freeze to help them survive at the Poles. Warm-blooded animals such as seals and polar bears generate their own heat by burning up food.

Seals are insulated from the icy polar temperatures by a thick layer of blubber.

Three kinds of Antarctic animal

Crab-eater Seal

Adelie Penguins

Emperor Penguin

How often do penguins fly?

They never fly at all. Their wings are so well adapted for swimming, that they are no longer any use for flying. Underwater, the penguin sculls along, using its wings like a pair of oars on a rowing boat.

Why do penguins stand upright?

Their legs are placed well back on their bodies, because they have to act as rudders underwater, and they work best if they are at the back. So when they are on land, penguins have to stand upright, unlike a sparrow or robin.

How deep do penguins dive?

Over 250 metres has been recorded for the Emperor Penguin.

What do Crabeater Seals eat?

Not crabs! Like many Antarctic animals they eat krill, the tiny shrimp-like animals that are found in enormous numbers in the Antarctic seas. The Crabeater Seal has specialized five-pointed teeth which mesh together to form a sieve-like structure. The seal takes a mouthfull of krill-rich water, then spits the water out through its teeth, which hold the krill back. Krill is also the main food of penguins and the baleen whales.

What was the Antarctic like 70 million years ago?

Amazingly, it was warm and covered by forest. There were many animals living there, including the ancestors of the Australian marsupials. At the time, Antarctica was joined up to South America on one side, and to Australia on the other. When these other continents broke away, and the climate became colder, Antarctica turned into an icy wasteland. The memory of this warm past is still below the ice, preserved as fossils.

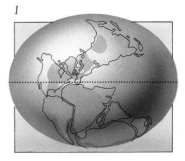

1

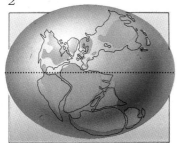

2

The Earth 400 (1), 100 (2) and 60 (3) million years ago

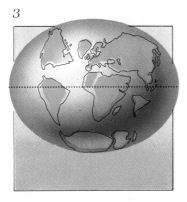

3

99

Blue Whale (top)
Sperm Whale (middle)
Right Whale (bottom)

Why don't whales have fur?

Because it would slow them down when they were swimming – if you swam with your clothes on you would be slowed down in just the same way.

Which seabirds are totally white?

Many seabirds have predominantly white plumage, though only the Ivory Gull and Fairy and Arctic Terns are pure white.

Where is the world's fastest swimming bird found?

In the Antarctic and South Atlantic Ocean. The record-holder is the Gentoo Penguin, which can swim at up to 43 kilometres per hour.

Why are there many more land animals in the Arctic than the Antarctic?

Because the Arctic is linked to land masses farther south, in Alaska, Greenland and Siberia. These links are partly by land and partly by sea ice in the winter. They allow animals to move backwards and forwards, going southwards below the Arctic Circle in the winter, and coming back into the High Arctic in summer. If they could not move south in the winter, they would not be able to survive there.

Which animal chews at the Antarctic ice?

The Weddell Seal. It keeps its breathing holes open during the severe Antarctic winter by chewing at the rim of the hole. In this way, Weddell Seals can live under the ice floes in winter. They live farther south than any other mammal, apart from Man. The Weddell Seals' teeth wear down eventually, and they die early as a result, living only half as long, on average, as other large seals.

What is tundra?

Tundra is a special type of low, scrubby vegetation found bordering the ice-covered regions of the Arctic. The top layer of soil thaws in summer, but below is a permanent layer of ice (*permafrost*). Water cannot drain away, so the surface is covered in pools all summer. Millions of flying insects, such as mosquitoes, breed here, and provide food for many birds, such as ducks, geese and waders. These birds fly thousands of miles to breed on the tundra every summer.

The Mountains

Why does the chinchilla have such thick fur?

Chinchillas are large rodents that live high up in the Andes mountains in South America. They can exist up to a height of nearly 7000 metres and have developed a thick furry coat to combat the extreme cold found at those altitudes. The South American Indians made warm winter clothes from the rich fur, and these were copied by the first Europeans to arrive in South America. Soon chinchilla fur became fashionable in Europe and numbers in the wild fell alarmingly. Since the 1930s numbers have risen again as chinchillas have been bred in captivity. This sturdy animal can get all the water it needs from licking the dew from local plants.

What is a Lammergeier?

A large and impressive bird of prey, related to the vultures. It inhabits mountain ranges in Africa, India, Tibet and southern Europe. The Lammergeier feeds on carrion, often picking over carcasses that other vultures have finished with. A true mountain bird, the Lammergeier has thickly feathered legs.

Which woodpecker never sees a tree?

The Andean Flicker, which spends its whole life above the tree-line, in the Andean mountains. It feeds on insects which it finds on the ground.

How would you sort the wild sheep from the wild goats?

Wild sheep generally have curled, blunt horns, and in the males these can be very large. Among wild goats, the horns are short and sharp, and about the same size in both sexes. Goats are adapted for life in rocky, barren places. They escape from predators by moving surefootedly over difficult, mountainous terrain which slows their enemies down. Most species of sheep are suited to life on the plains.

What is the world's largest bird of prey?

The Andean Condor, a vulture-like bird whose bare head has a strange flattish lump above the beak, rather like a beret falling over its eyes. It feeds on a mixture of carrion and live prey. Although most Andean Condors live high up in the mountains, some are found on cliffs by the sea.

What is a Mountain Beaver?

Not a beaver at all, but a large rodent with a short, stubby body and almost no tail. What is more, it does not live in mountains! This secretive, solitary rodent is found in damp forests of the north-western USA. How it got its inappropriate name is anybody's guess.

Why do so many types of goat live on mountains?

Goats are well suited to mountain life. Their hoofs are specially adapted for gripping rocks, giving them a supreme ability to clamber up mountainsides. Their thick coats keep out the cold. And they can eat virtually anything, which is useful when food is scarce.

Mountain goats, such as this Ibex have pointed hoofs that help them to climb steep slopes.

Why are so many eagles and other birds of prey found on mountains?

Birds of prey can live in almost any habitat, but they like mountains for several reasons. Many use upward currents of air to make flying easy. The lack of trees and sparse vegetation make feeding simpler, because prey animals can be spotted on the ground. Equally important is that in the mountains there are few humans to hunt and persecute birds of prey.

Eagle

Which insects live above the snow-line and what do they eat?

The grylloblattids, a strange order of insects that are probably a 'missing link' between the cockroaches and the crickets. They live on snowfields in the Canadian Rockies. Grylloblattids feed on dead or dying insects from the lower slopes of the mountains, which are carried up by air currents and then deposited on the snow.

What is a Wallcreeper?

A grey bird with red wings, found on rocky cliffs in mountainous areas of Europe and Asia. It feeds by clinging close to the rock face and shuffling slowly upwards, searching every nook and cranny for insects. When it gets to the top it flies down to the bottom again, and starts working upwards on a new section of cliff. The Wallcreeper is related to the nuthatches which search tree trunks and branches for insects, working in a similar way.

Northern Forests

Where would you find a Twig Caterpillar?

You would be very lucky to find one at all, but you could try looking in any tree or bush. These caterpillars are so well disguised as twigs that they are very difficult to find, unless they happen to move. Knobbly, brown, and marked like twigs, they perfect their disguise by holding themselves stiffly at an angle to a larger twig.

Why do woodpeckers peck wood?

For several different reasons. They feed on insects which burrow in wood and under bark. They also nest in trees, and sometimes peck out holes for themselves if they cannot find a suitable nest hole. Finally, some woodpeckers drum their beaks loudly against trees to attract a mate. One species, the acorn woodpecker, drills holes just for food storage. It makes hundreds of acorn-sized holes in trees or telegraph poles and stores an acorn in each one.

Acorn Woodpecker

Green Woodpecker

Where does the Green Woodpecker find most of its food?

On the ground. Ants are one of its main foods, although it does peck trees for wood-boring insects as well. Green Woodpeckers also use trees to spy out the surrounding land for ant hills. And like other woodpeckers, they nest in trees.

Which bird has a beak that can prise open pine cones?

The aptly named crossbill. Few other birds can break through the hard wood of a cone to get at its seeds. The two halves of its beak are curved at the tip, and cross over each other. The bird pushes its beak in between the scales of a cone, then moves the lower part of the beak sideways, at the same time twisting its head. This action splits the cone scale in two so that the bird can pull out the seed beneath.

Why are the sapsuckers wrongly named?

Because they do not *suck* sap, but lap it up with their tongues. The sapsuckers are two unusual species of woodpecker found only in North and Central America. In spring, they drill holes in the trunks of deciduous trees, such as maples and apples, just when the sap is rising. The sap oozes out of the holes, and the sapsuckers return at intervals to drink it up. Insects are also attracted to the nutritious sap, and the sapsuckers eat these too.

Where do treecreepers nest?

Under the bark of trees. They look for some loose bark then squeeze behind it to create a crevice for their tiny nest.

Which animals actually live inside the leaves of trees?

The larvae of insects known as Leaf Miners. These include various moths and flies, which lay their eggs in the leaves of certain plants. The larva moves around the leaf, eating out a winding passage-way, which can be seen on the leaf surface as a pale, wiggly line.

How did the Snowshoe Hare get its name?

The name comes from its huge feet with their fringe of dense fur. These act as snowshoes, to prevent the hare from sinking into deep snow drifts in winter. Snowshoe Hares live in coniferous forests of Alaska and northern Canada where winters are long and cold.

Snowshoe Hare

Grasslands

Why are vultures found mainly in grasslands?

Because they feed on the carcasses of large animals. These are much easier to find in grasslands than in forest or scrub where the ground is difficult to see from the air. Vultures and condors (which have the same way of life) also do well in mountainous regions and on the fringes of deserts. Here they can soar high in the air, keeping a lookout for their next meal.

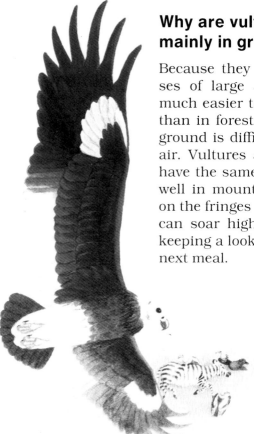

Vulture

Why do vultures have naked heads?

Because they often feed by pushing their heads inside carcasses, to get at the soft flesh inside. This leaves their heads covered with blood. Because they are unfeathered, their heads are easier to keep clean.

Which bird nests in the old burrows of Prairie Dogs?

The Burrowing Owl, a small owl that stands only 25 centimetres tall. The owls will not share the burrows with Prairie Dogs, but take them over once they are abandoned. Sometimes several owls share a large burrow. These little owls have long legs, and are quite efficient excavators themselves. They often enlarge the burrow to suit their needs, and hollow out a nesting chamber.

What do oxpeckers eat?

The ticks and other parasites that infest grazing mammals on the African savannah. Because they are largely beneficial, mammals such as buffalo and rhinoceroses tolerate the oxpeckers and allow them to feed undisturbed. oxpeckers also peck at cuts and sores, and may sometimes do the mammals more harm than good, by opening up the wounds to infection.

What sort of animal is a Prairie Dog?

A rodent – a relative of the rats and mice. Prairie Dogs live together in large underground colonies, known as 'townships'. There may be several thousand animals in a single colony, and the ground is riddled with burrows. The Prairie Dogs get their name from their sharp, bark-like cry.

Prairie Dogs live together in great networks of underground tunnels.

Which large grassland mammal is a 'living fossil'?

The pronghorn of North America, which has unique branched horns. It is often referred to as an antelope, but is not a member of that group; antelope all have unbranched horns. The pronghorn also sheds its horns each year, which antelope do not. Neither is the pronghorn a deer, but a member of an ancient family most of which died out over 10 million years ago.

What do the ostrich and the rhea have in common?

Both are long-legged, flightless, fast-running birds that live in open grasslands – but they are found on different continents. The rhea is a South American bird, while the ostrich is from southern Africa. It is no coincidence that they live in such similar habitats. Where there are no trees to perch in, flight is of little use. Instead, these large birds run from danger.

Where would you find wild hamsters?

On the steppes, a type of grassland found in arid regions of Asia and the Middle East. Because food is often scarce in their dry homelands, hamsters have storage pouches in their cheeks – so that when they find a rich source of plant seeds they can take some away to store in their burrow.

What is a boomslang?

A boomslang is a poisonous tree-dwelling snake from the African savannah. Its grooved fangs, down which the poison runs, are located towards the back of the jaw.

Which grassland animal gives birth to young that are almost as large as itself?

The Tsetse Fly (pronounced 'tetsy' fly) of the African savannahs. It keeps its single egg inside its body, until the egg has hatched. Then the fly gives birth to a fat, legless, white larva that is almost as large as its own body.

The pronghorn's closest relative is an extinct prehistoric ancestor.

Can cows and horses digest grass?

No, not without help. Grass, like other plants, is made up mainly of a tough substance called *cellulose*. Digesting cellulose is difficult, and very few animals can manage to do this. Humans cannot, which is why leafy foods such as lettuce and cabbage do not make us fat. The animals that eat grass, such as cows and horse, have special bacteria living inside them which *can* digest cellulose. These bacteria digest the grass, and turn it into a nutritious food for the cows and horses. The same is true of all the wild grassland animals, such as antelopes, deer, giraffes, rhinoceroses and zebras. Some, such as cows and deer, have the bacteria living in their stomachs. Others, such as zebras and horses, have the bacteria living in their intestines.

How did the Leopard Tortoise get its name?

Not by being fast and ferocious, but by having a shell that looks something like a leopard's coat. With its mottled, yellow-and-black shell, the leopard tortoise is well camouflaged on the dry African savannahs where it lives. This tortoise is a vegetarian, feeding on grass, leaves and fruit. Such a diet provides little calcium – the hard mineral that tortoises need for their shells. So the Leopard Tortoise gnaws at old, dry bones to get the calcium it needs.

Which South American wolf has unusually long legs?

The long legs of the Maned Wolf give it an elegant appearance. It is a shy, nocturnal creature and feeds mainly on insects, small mammals and fruit.

Which birds become prisoners in their own nests?

Female hornbills, which are walled into their nests with mud collected by the male hornbill. All species of hornbill do this, and most are found on the wooded savannahs of Africa. The male continues to feed the female and her chicks through a slit left in the mud wall. During her imprisonment, the female moults and is completely featherless for most of the time. Her feathers regrow by the time she breaks out of the nest. The chicks then rebuild the barricade, and both parents collect food for them until they are ready to leave the nest. Becoming a prisoner in the nest protects the hornbill and her chicks from predators.

Hornbills

What does a flamingo have in common with a Blue Whale?

They both catch their prey by filtering it from water. The Blue Whale has a sieve made of elongated teeth, known as baleen. The flamingo has a similar sieving structure inside its large beak. The two also eat similar food – both rely on small shrimp-like crustaceans that live in the water in huge numbers.

How many bison once roamed the North American prairie?

No one knows for sure how many of these splendid beasts once grazed the prairie – some say 30 million, others say twice as many again. Their senseless slaughter by European settlers during the 19th century brought them to the brink of extinction.

What is a Zorilla?

The African equivalent of a skunk. It is long and sleek, beautifully patterned in black and white, with a fine bushy tail. But its smell is anything but beautiful. Like the skunk, the Zorilla produces this repulsive odour to deter its enemies. Zorillas live on the African savannah feeding on small mammals, lizards, birds' eggs and insects.

Zorillas, when threatened, emit a vile odour.

Deserts

Are the Kit Fox and Fennec Fox related?

Although these large-eared foxes look similar and lead similar life styles, they are not related. Kit Foxes inhabit the deserts of North America, while Fennec Foxes are confined to arid regions of northern Africa. Both sleep in burrows during the day, and both come out at night to feed on rodents, insects, birds and lizards. They provide a good example of convergent evolution – when unrelated animals develop similar features to cope with similar habitats.

Where does the Elf Owl nest?

Inside the stems of large cactus plants. This tiny owl is found in the deserts of Mexico and the southern United States. In the breeding season it looks for holes in cacti where it can built its nest.

Where would you find a Thorny Devil?

The deserts of Australia. The Thorny Devil is a remarkably prickly lizard which keeps predators at bay with its thorn-covered skin.

Condensed dew on the spines of the Thorny Devil provide it with a useful source of water.

In what ways have gerbils adapted to desert life?

Gerbils are seed-eating rodents of Asia and Africa which are perfectly adapted to living in deserts. Resting in burrows during the day to avoid the sun's glare, they emerge at dusk to forage for seeds. They eke out an existence on comparatively little food, and are extraordinarily efficient at reducing water loss from their bodies. Their kidneys produce very concentrated urine, and the bones in their noses are adapted to condense water vapour from the air they breathe out. They have long hind legs to keep as much distance as possible between their bodies and the hot sand, and the soles of their feet are protected by thick pads of fur.

What is a sandfish?

A type of lizard, found in the deserts of Saudi Arabia. It is called a sandfish because it moves through the sand, beneath the surface, with a swimming motion. It feeds on insects that it finds in the sand.

Why do desert rodents have white bellies?

Many desert rodents have white bellies to reflect the radiant heat given out by the sand. Gerbils, jerboas and Kangaroo Rats all share this feature.

Which animal has eyelids that act as sunshades?

The Lake Eyre Dragon, a small lizard found on the barren salt-pans of Lake Eyre in South Australia. The temperature here can sometimes reach 60°C and the sun shines harshly down on the brilliant white wastes. The Lake Eyre Dragon's eyelids stick out horizontally, shielding the eyes, just like sunshades.

Can frogs live in deserts?

Surprisingly, they can. Many desert areas have some frogs that spend most of their time in a state of dormancy, or suspended animation, deep underground. They enclose themselves in a waterproof membrane, or a cocoon of mud, to retain their body moisture. These desert frogs only emerge from this dormant state when it rains to mate and lay eggs.

Where do budgerigars come from?

Wild budgerigars come from the Australian outback, and when conditions are favourable, flocks of these pretty birds can be quite commonplace. Although the caged birds come in many different colours, the plumage of the wild budgerigar is nearly always green.

Why is the Golden Mole blind?

Because it hunts beneath the sand in the Namib Desert in southern Africa, 'swimming' along beneath the surface and rarely coming above ground. Eyes are delicate, and easily damaged by the moving sand particles. Since vision is not much use to the Golden Mole anyway, natural selection has favoured the complete loss of the eyes. Instead it has a superb sense of touch and vibration.

How does the Kangaroo Rat survive without drinking?

So efficient are the kidneys of this American desert rat that it never has to drink. All the liquid it needs is extracted from the seeds it eats.

Which birds carry water in their breast feathers?

Sandgrouse, birds which inhabit dry and desert ares throughout Africa and the Middle East. The males have the special breast feathers that allow them to pick up water. These have a coiled structure when dry, but can open out when wet, expanding as they do so. This allows them to soak up water like a sponge. The males use their feathers to carry water to their chicks.

Sandgrouse

Islands

Why do so many flightless birds live on islands?

Because islands that are far out in the ocean rarely have large mammals on them. These islands were formed by volcanoes and were completely bare of life at first. The only animals found there are those that can fly, or survive a long ocean journey floating on a log. This means there are no large predators to pose a threat to birds. So birds could lose the power of flight and still be safe. Many flightless birds have developed other defences such as powerful legs for running and kicking.

A skeleton of the giant flightless moa from New Zealand, now extinct.

Where would you find a meat-eating parrot?

In only one place in the world – New Zealand. The carnivorous parrot, known as a Kea, has a sharply hooked beak and lives in wild, open country. It is one of the many unusual birds to be found in New Zealand. Although fairly close to Australia, New Zealand is cut off from it by treacherous ocean currents. These effectively prevented any mammals reaching the islands, apart from some bats. In the absence of mammals, birds evolved in many unusual ways, producing flightless giants such as the moas, now extinct, and smaller flightless birds like the Kiwi.

Why did the dodo become extinct?

Because it was very tame and unafraid of humans. Sailors found it easy to kill the birds and stock their ships up with meat. Eventually, the dodos died out as a result. Tameness is common among island birds, because they have not evolved alongside predatory mammals, and had little to fear before the arrival of people.

Where are lemurs found?

On Madagascar, and nowhere else on Earth. Lemurs are an ancient group of animals, related to the ancestors of the monkeys and apes. They are less intelligent than the monkeys, and died out in most parts of the world, as the monkeys evolved and took over their habitats. Only in Madagascar did the lemurs survive, because the monkeys never reached this island.

Ring-tailed Lemurs

The tenrec, a primitive insect-eating mammal.

What is a tenrec?

A type of small mammal found only in Madagascar and the Comoro Islands. There are 30 species of tenrec, some resembling shrews, others looking remarkably like hedgehogs. They all eat insects and other invertebrates, filling the role that insectivores have in other parts of the world. Tenrecs are quite primitive mammals, with some features like the reptiles from which mammals evolved.

Why were the Galapagos Islands so important to Charles Darwin?

Because islands like the Galapagos, far out in the ocean, act as 'evolutionary experiments'. Only a few animals manage to reach them, so evolution often follows a different course here. Animals like the Galapagos finches and giant tortoises were, for Darwin, examples of evolution in action.

Where would you find a cricket the size of a mouse and a fly the size of a butterfly?

In New Zealand, the home of many strange and unique creatures. Because it has no native mammals, apart from bats, other animals have evolved in unusual ways. The cricket, known as a Giant Weta, can measure up to 10 centimetres in length, and weigh as much as 80 grams. It takes the place of mice and shrews, eating leaves and insects. Much less is known about the Giant Fly, which has a body about five centimetres long and huge butterfly-like wings.

Why are there no snakes in Ireland?

Because Ireland was mostly covered by glaciers during the Ice Age. The southern coast was ice-free, but too cold for snakes to survive. As the Ice Age ended, snakes migrated northwards through Europe, and some reached Britain before the rising sea levels cut it off from France. But they did not manage to reach Ireland before the sea cut it off.

Where are flightless rails found?

On many different islands, including New Zealand, New Guinea, Laysan Island, Aldabra, Tristan da Cunha, Gough Island and Inaccessible Island. Of all the rails living on islands, one in four are flightless. Rails obviously evolve into flightless forms with great ease. They do this by a process called *neoteny*, in which they become sexually mature without 'growing up' physically.

Which other islands, apart from the Galapagos, have Giant Tortoises?

Aldabra Island, in the Indian Ocean. There were once Giant Tortoises on other Indian Ocean islands, but these died out long ago, as a result of over-hunting by sailors.

Tropical Forests

Spider Monkeys move effortlessly through the tree tops.

Which forest animal has five legs?

None, but the Spider Monkeys of South America are sometimes said to have a 'fifth limb', because of the remarkable way they use their tails when moving about in the trees. These tails can curl right around a branch, and support the animal's full weight. So a Spider Monkey can swing upside down from a branch by its tail as it reaches out with its hands to gather food. The tail has a rough leathery patch on the underside to give it a more secure grip.

Which frog rears its tadpoles inside a plant?

Several different types of Amazonian tree frogs do this, using plants called bromeliads as a nursery. Bromeliads grow high up on the branches of trees. Their leaves are arranged in a circle to form a cup-like hollow where rainwater can collect. The parent frog guards its eggs on the damp forest floor, or carries the eggs about until they hatch. Once they have hatched, the adult frog transfers the tadpoles to the bromeliad.

Which bird has trouble sitting on its eggs because its tail is so long?

The Quetzal of Central America. The male of this species has tail feathers that are 61 centimetres long, twice as long as its body. It takes its turn at brooding the eggs, which are laid in a tree hole, often one abandoned by a woodpecker. When sitting on the eggs, facing out of the hole, the male Quetzal's tail feathers are folded over its head and stick out of the entrance. By the time the breeding season is over, these long plumes no longer look their best and are replaced.

Flying Foxes are large fruit-eating bats. Their 'wings', supported on long fingers measure 1.5 metres wide.

Why does a toucan have such a large, brightly coloured beak?

No one is quite sure, but the toucan's bill seems to help it in various ways. Because it is so long it can be used for reaching fruit that is hanging at the end of a branch. Toucans also eat the nestlings of other birds, and the huge, garish beak seems to make the toucan look more frightening, so that parent birds do not try to fight it off from the nest.

What type of animal is a flying fox?

A large fruit-eating bat. There are over 170 species of flying fox, and unlike most bats they have large eyes and long muzzles. It is their fox-like faces that led to the name 'flying fox'. They fly at dusk in search of fruit, relying mainly on sight and smell to find their way. flying foxes are found in Asia, Africa, Australia and the islands of the Pacific.

Where do the trees light up at night?

In parts of southeast Asia, where male fireflies gather in particular trees to flash their messages to the females. By getting together and flashing their lights in time with each other, they can attract females from a much wider area.

What do chimpanzees and gorillas eat?

Gorillas, despite their great size, are mainly vegetarian. Their diet consists of leaves, bark, and some berries. Chimpanzees have a much more varied menu. In addition to leaves and fruit, they eat insects and birds' eggs. They also hunt other animals, such as young monkeys and bushpigs.

Chimpanzee

Which animal's name means 'old man of the forest'?

The orang-utan of Sumatra and Borneo. The adult males have a solemn, elderly look caused by heavy flaps of blackish skin all round the face, and a fringe of rust-coloured fur that resembles a beard.

Orang-utan

Three-toed Sloth

Which animal is camouflaged by the algae growing in its fur?

The Three-toed Sloth. Unlike most mammals, it does not keep its fur scrupulously clean. In fact, each outer hair has a grooved surface which encourages algae (single-celled plants) to grow in the grooves. The algae give the sloth's fur a greenish tinge. So when it is hanging motionless in the branches (as it usually is) with its head tucked in between its arms, the sloth looks just like a mass of lichen or moss growing on the branch. This protects the sloth from predators.

What is a linsang?

A slender agile animal, rather like a long, thin cat, but with a pointed, mouse-like nose and very short legs. Linsangs live among the branches of tropical forests, eating insects, young birds and fruit. The African linsang is a beautiful cream colour with dark brown spots on the body and brown stripes all along the tail. Other species of linsang are similar in colour, but with more stripes than spots.

How do Flower Mantids catch their prey?

By being disguised as a flower and catching flying insects that come in search of nectar. They have elaborately disguised legs that are extended and flattened in graceful petal-like shapes. When positioned among flowers of a matching shade they are almost invisible.

Goliath Birdwing butterfly

What is a Goliath Birdwing?

An enormous butterfly, found in the forests of New Guinea, with a wingspan of up to 21 centimetres. The male is dressed in a dazzling pattern of black and metallic green, while the female is only slightly less colourful. Despite its name, the Goliath is not the largest butterfly of all. Its close relative, the Queen Alexandra's Birdwing, can reach a wingspan of 28 centimetres.

Do Flying Lemurs fly?

No, but they are among the most accomplished gliding animals. A Flying Lemur has very large flaps of skin connecting its neck to its forelimbs, its forelimbs to its hindlimbs, and its hindlimbs to its long tail. In flight, its outstretched flying membrane makes it look more like a kite than an animal. A Flying Lemur, which is only a distant relation of the true lemurs, can glide for up to 135 metres between trees. It climbs well, but because it is so well adapted for gliding it is unable to move on the ground.

Which are the noisiest animals in the Amazon forest?

The aptly named Howler Monkeys. There are six different species found in the forests of South and Central America, and their cries can be heard over a kilometre away, even in dense jungle. Howlers have an enlarged bone in the throat which is hollow. As air is forced through this hole it produces the ear-splitting howl. Males are much noisier than females, thanks to a larger hyoid bone.

How many different species live in the rainforest?

Estimates vary between 2 million and over 20 million. All the bird and mammal species are probably known, and so are most trees, reptiles and amphibians. But the insects can only be estimated by discovering how many unique ones there are in each type of tree.

What is unusual about Army Ants and Driver Ants?

Unlike other ants, their nests are not permanent. The colony is nomadic, moving on at regular intervals. When they do stop, Army Ants form a temporary nest from their own bodies, inside which the queen produces her eggs. On the move, Army Ants consume anything and everything. After they have passed through a stretch of rainforest, there are few insects or other creatures left in the undergrowth, and it can take weeks or even months for the animals to re-establish themselves.

Where would you find the world's only nocturnal monkey?

In the South American rainforest. This small monkey is known simply as the Night Monkey. Unlike most nocturnal animals it can see in colour, and it cannot move about easily on moonless nights.

Why do antbirds follow columns of Army Ants?

Because they find most of their food in this way. The Army Ants are voracious creatures that try to eat everything in their path. Some insects, such as cockroaches, and spiders, are large enough and fast enough to escape the advancing ants. But as they attempt to flee, the antbirds snap them up.

A column of Army Ants

The Seashore

What do lugworms eat?

Lugworms eat sand which they enrich with organic particles. To do this they dig a U-shaped mine shaft and pump water through one of the shafts to trap particles within a sandy plug. The waste product is seen as coiled castings on the beach.

A turtle returns to the sea after laying eggs on the beach.

Male and female Shovelers

How does a Shoveler feed?

The Shoveler is a medium-sized duck that lives in freshwater marshes and estuaries in Europe. It is the only duck to have a huge spatula-like beak. This is used as a shovel, to strain tiny plants and animals from the water. It nests in lined hollows near the water's edge.

Where do kittiwakes lay their eggs?

Kittiwakes spend most of their lives flying over the oceans of the northern hemisphere: they only venture ashore to breed. Vast colonies of birds may be observed nesting on exposed cliffs, often in the company of guillemots. Kittiwakes build high-sided nests of grass, seaweed and guano (birds' droppings), which they cement to the cliff with mud. Both parents take turns in incubating the eggs.

What is a wendletrap?

A wendletrap is a beautiful shell which is occasionally washed up on the seashore. Its name derives from the Dutch word meaning 'spiral staircase'.

What is a stargazer?

A fish whose large, upturned eyes look as if they are staring at the heavens. Because its eyes are in the top of its head, the stargazer can bury the rest of its body in the sandy sea bed. Disguised in this way, it ambushes smaller fish, stunning them with a mild electric shock from organs just behind its eyes.

What is the connection between barnacle geese and goose barnacles?

None at all, except in the minds of medieval people. Because geese only appeared on European shores in winter, no one knew where they laid their eggs. But they found certain long-stalked barnacles attached to driftwood on the shore, near the geese. To an imaginative mind, these look like legless geese, upside down. The story grew up that the barnacles were the embryos of geese, which hatched on trees then dropped into the water and turned into adult geese. The barnacles were called 'goose barnacles' as a result, and the geese, 'barnacle geese'.

What is a skimmer?

It is an American bird with an unusual way of catching fish. The lower half of its beak is much longer than the upper half, and it flies low over the sea, beak open, with the lower beak just breaking the water. As soon as it feels a fish, the beak snaps shut with the fish inside.

What is the only marine insect?

The only insects to live in contact with the sea are Marine Springtails. They do not actually live in seawater but on the surface of it, usually on rock pools or small puddles left behind by the retreating tide. The bodies of these springtails are covered with a mat of fine hairs which trap a layer of air around them. If washed away by the tide, they can survive for up to five days just by breathing this trapped air.

What is a Sea Potato?

A type of sea urchin, covered with golden-brown spines. It lives buried in the sandy sea-bed, eating tiny particles of waste that it scrapes from the surface of sand grains. The animal does not really look much like a potato. The name refers to the empty shell which has no spines and could be mistaken for a potato.

Is the Sea Hare a mammal?

No, it is a type of sea slug. It is called a sea hare, although it is never more than 20 centimetres long, because it is brown and has two long sensory tentacles on the top of its head, that look something like the ears of a hare. Sea hares live among seaweeds on the lower part of the shore.

Why is the Mudskipper an unusual fish?

This strange little fish lives in coastal waters of tropical Africa, around mangrove swamps. At low tide, Mudskippers haul themselves up out of the water to hunt small prey on the bare mud. They can 'walk' quite well and even climb the mangrove roots, using a single 'foot' formed from their front fins to pull themselves forward.

Do dolphins drink seawater?

Yes. Their kidneys are much more effective at removing salts and concentrating them in their urine, so they are not killed by drinking seawater as we would be.

How did the Wrybill get its name?

From its oddly shaped beak, which is curved to one side. The Wrybill finds its food by turning over stones on the shore, and looking for small invertebrates underneath. Its bill is ideally shaped for this.

A colourful Sea Hare

Why does the Furrow Shell breathe through long tubes?

Because it lives buried in the mud, where there is little oxygen. Like other molluscs that bury themselves, it has two long tubes extending upwards to the sea bed. One draws in water, from which the mollusc extracts food particles as well as oxygen. The other tube takes waste water back to the surface.

The Oceans

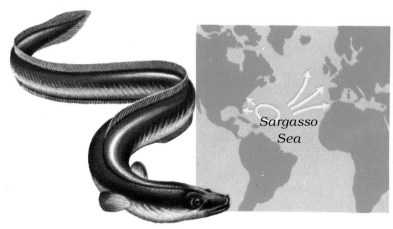

Where do flatfish live?

On the sea bed, usually where there is sand or small pebbles. Because they are so flat, and have a speckled pattern like the seabed, they are very well camouflaged.

What sort of animal is a 'windowpane'?

A flatfish, found off the eastern coast of North America. It was given its odd name by fishermen, because it has such a thin body that it provides very little food.

What is a Leatherback?

A type of turtle. Instead of the hard, bony shell of other turtles, it has a shell that feels like stiff rubber or leather. The shell is soft because of the lack of calcium (chalk) in its diet. It also has no claws and no scales. The leatherback is the world's largest turtle, and it feeds mainly on jellyfish, which are plentiful in all tropical oceans.

A turtle hatching from its egg. Leatherback Turtles' eggs have soft, leathery shells.

Eels breed in the Atlantic and swim to America and Europe.

Which animals travel thousands of kilometres to the Sargasso Sea to breed?

Freshwater eels from Europe and North America. In an astonishing test of endurance, they move from freshwater to saltwater, then swim as much as 5000 kilometres to the Sargasso Sea. This 'sea' is nothing more than a mass of seaweed adrift in the Atlantic Ocean. The young eels have never visited it before, but they find it by instinct alone. Their eggs hatch into tiny larvae that slowly drift back to the rivers of Europe or North America, taking up to three years in the case of the European eel. After spawning, the adult eels are thought to die.

What is a Mermaid's Purse?

The egg-case of a dogfish or skate. The case is tough and leathery with a long tendril at each corner. After the eggs have been laid, these tendrils can bind to seaweeds to anchor the egg-case in shallow water. There is just one egg inside. It has a large yolk on which the young fish is nourished, and eight to nine months pass before the fish emerges from the case.

What is the largest invertebrate and why does it live in the sea?

The Giant Squid, which is known to reach 21 metres in length and may even grow longer. No land invertebrate could reach this size, because air does not support an animal's body as well as water. It is no coincidence that the world's largest vertebrate, the Blue Whale, also lives in the sea.

Do Killer Whales attack people?

No. These large predatory whales will attack many large animals, even those many times their size. But they have never been known to attack human beings.

Killer Whales are not dangerous to humans.

What are gills and which animals have them?

They are feathery structures that can extract oxygen from water. Fish have them, and so do many other animals that live in water. These include molluscs such as mussels and squid, shrimps, sea urchins, tadpoles and ragworms. In some animals the gills can be seen, but in most they are hidden from view in an internal chamber, through which water can pass.

Can squid hear?

Tests show that some species of squid have little or no sense of hearing. This may be because squid are preyed on by dolphins, which use very loud blasts of low-frequency sound to capture their prey. By damaging their sensitive organs of hearing, the sound stuns the prey briefly, and before it recovers the dolphins move in for the kill. Squid without any organs of hearing are less vulnerable to the dolphins. Their other sense organs are well developed, especially their eyes, to compensate for complete lack of hearing.

Squid

What is the slowest growing animal on Earth?

A Deep-sea Clam, which only grows to about eight millimetres, but takes over 90 years to reach this size.

Which fish use bacteria to help them catch their prey?

The Flashlight Fish, which are found in tropical seas. Under each eye they have large round sacs, which give out a powerful light – hence their name. But they do not produce the light themselves. The sacs contain millions of light-producing bacteria, which illuminate the sea for them. In return, the fish provide the bacteria with food. Flashlight fish use their powerful lights in several ways, including searching out the smaller animals on which they feed. The lights also act as lures. Other fish come to investigate, only to be eaten by the Flashlight Fish.

What is plankton?

Plankton is made up of thousands of different microscopic creatures that float at the surface of the ocean. Some of these creatures are tiny one-celled plants, which make food using the light from the Sun. Others are tiny animals, which feed on those plants. The plants are known as 'phytoplankton' and the animals as 'zooplankton'. The phytoplankton are the forests and meadows of the ocean – they make all the food to keep the ocean's animals alive. Although you cannot see most of the planktonic creatures, they are the most important inhabitants of the ocean.

Where do sea snakes lay their eggs?

Nowhere. The female keeps the eggs inside her body until they have hatched into young snakes. The ocean is a very dangerous place for eggs. There are few places to hide them, and many hungry mouths ready to swallow them up. Ocean animals cope with this in two main ways. They either produce millions of eggs and release them freely, relying on a few surviving to hatch. Or they guard their eggs inside their bodies, as do sea snakes, sharks and some other fish.

How did the Storm Petrels get their name?

They are named after St Peter, who tried to walk on the water. Storm Petrels feed on small fish and squid taken from the surface waters. Some catch their food by flying low over the surface, with their feet 'pattering' on the sea as if they were walking on it. Other types of petrel do not feed in this way, but because they are related to Storm Petrels they acquired the same name.

Which snail travels the oceans attached to a raft of bubbles?

The purple or violet sea snail, *Janthina*. It produces a sticky mucus which it blows into a mass of bubbles. These form a float from which the snail hangs upside down, just below the surface. There it is ideally placed to feed on small creatures in the surface waters. The wind blows the raft along, so the snail moves effortlessly from one part of the ocean to another.

A parrot fish, clearly showing the 'beak'.

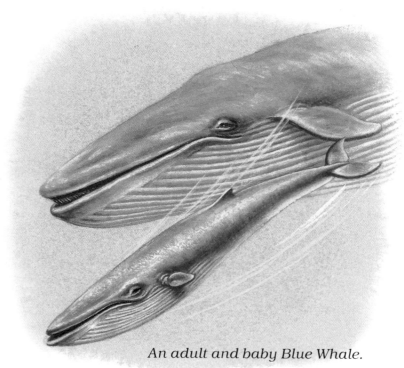

An adult and baby Blue Whale.

What is the fastest-growing animal on Earth?

A baby Blue Whale. From a fertilized egg, too small to see, it grows to three tonnes at birth (about 11 or 12 months later) and then to 25 tonnes after another year. For the first six or seven months after birth, it lives on the thick, nutritious milk of the mother whale.

Can Giant Clams drown swimmers by trapping their legs?

No, this is one of the great myths about animals. Giant Clams, like most shelled molluscs, are slow-moving creatures. Their shells only close very slowly, and would be incapable of trapping someone's leg unless they had actually fallen asleep.

Where would you find parrotfish?

Among coral reefs. These fish are so called because they have two hard plates at the front of the mouth, formed from rows of teeth fused together. These plates act rather like a bird's beak, as the parrot-fish nibbles off pieces of living coral. In the parrot-fish's throat there are more teeth that grind the coral down. The fish can then digest the soft living part of the coral.

River Life

What is a Mudpuppy?

A type of amphibian, related to the salamanders. Mudpuppies are found only in North America, and unlike most amphibians they spend their whole lives in lakes and streams, never emerging on to land. For this reason, they keep their external gills to extract oxygen from the water. Most amphibians lose these gills during the tadpole stage.

Where would you find a pink dolphin?

In the River Amazon. Other river dolphins are grey or brown, but the Amazon Dolphin is a pale shell pink underneath, with a pale grey back. Like all river dolphins it has very poor eyesight, because the waters in which it lives are so murky with sediment. It relies heavily on echolocation to find its way about.

What is the largest freshwater fish?

The Giant Catfish of the Mekong River in southeast Asia. This rare and elusive animal can grow up to three metres long.

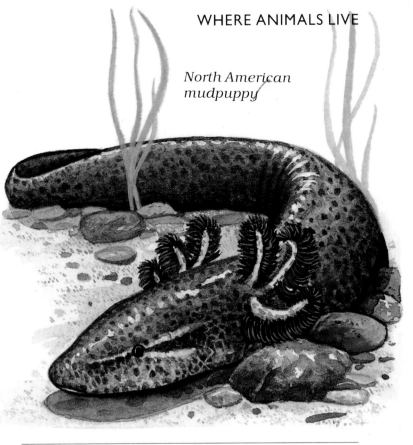

North American mudpuppy

Which animal carries its young in a waterproof pouch?

The Water Opossum of Central and South America. It is the only marsupial in the world to have taken to an aquatic way of life. A strong ring of muscle around the mouth of the pouch makes it waterproof when closed. The Water Opossum can carry up to five young with her when hunting for fish and crustaceans on the river bed.

Giant Catfish

Which animal has difficulty just staying in the same place?

The Torrent Duck of South America. This bird lives in the raging torrents of the Andes Mountains. The water flows so fast down the steep slopes, that the duck is constantly in danger of being washed away. To help it survive in this difficult environment, it has sharp claws on its toes, with which to grip underwater boulders, and a stiff tail to brace itself. The Torrent Duck is also a powerful swimmer, and can stay where it is by swimming hard against the current. What makes this difficult life worthwhile is the lack of competition from other waterbirds, which cannot cope with these conditions. Little or no competition means abundant food for the torrent duck.

What is unusual about the bird known as a Dipper?

Although it spends all its life in streams, the Dipper shows no obvious adaptations to a life in water, such as webbed feet. Charles Darwin remarked that if he had been shown a Dipper, without knowing anything of its habits, he would never have guessed it was a waterbird. The Dipper perches on rocks in fast-flowing streams, then darts into the water after its prey. It runs along the stream-bed, making flying movements with its wings, which propel it through the water. Darwin suspected that the Dipper had only recently evolved from an ancestor that was not aquatic – although its way of life had changed, natural selection had not yet had enough time to make changes to its body.

The Dipper is not properly adapted to its life in water.

Why are freshwater snails important to pond fish?

A healthy pond is a self-contained community of plants and animals, all living together in natural harmony. However, if something happens to upset this balance, then the whole community can be put at risk. For instance, freshwater snails help to keep the plants under control, and so maintain the balance of gases in the water.

Crayfish

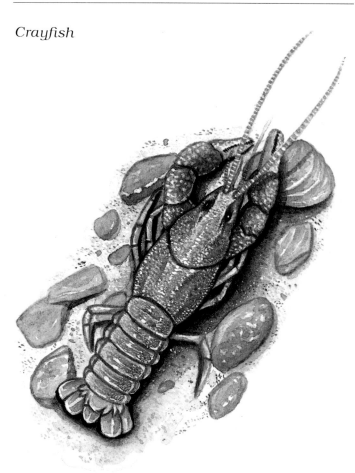

Is a crayfish a fish?

No, it is a large crustacean, a relative of the crabs and shrimps. There are more than 500 species of crayfish, which all live in streams and rivers. They are the freshwater equivalents of lobsters, but not as large. Because crayfish need plenty of calcium to make their thick external skeleton, they are mainly found in chalk streams. Nocturnal animals, they are rarely seen, only emerging after dark to feed on insect larvae, snails and tadpoles.

Ponds and Marshes

What is a hammerkop?

A hammerkop is an African marsh bird, whose head has a hammer-shaped profile. This all-brown bird, with its long beak and backward-pointing head crest, is perhaps best known for the huge nests it builds. Measuring up to two metres across and resting on the boughs of trees, these untidy structures of sticks and mud often provide homes to other animals.

Does the Walking Catfish really walk?

Yes, it can move over land, using its front fins as 'legs' to pull itself along, but it cannot raise its belly off the ground when it walks, as a true land animal can. The Walking Catfish lives in small ponds that dry up from time to time. When this happens, the fish has to go in search of a new pond. It produces a thick coat of mucus to prevent itself from drying out during the journey. As well as gills, it has small air-breathing sacs, which work in the same way as lungs.

Which birds have feathers that crumble into powder?

The herons, egrets and their relatives. Only a small number of their feathers do this – they are known as 'powder down', and they occur in patches on the breast. The birds spread the powder on to other feathers when preening themselves after a meal. It helps to absorb oil from the fish they eat and plays an important part in keeping the feathers clean.

What is a Water Measurer?

A pond-dwelling insect which is so slender it looks almost like a miniature stick insect. It weighs so little that it can walk on the surface of water without sinking. It is called a Water Measurer because it seems to be pacing out the water's surface.

Where does the Great Diving Beetle lay its eggs?

Inside the stems of waterlily leaves. The female beetle has a sharp ovipositor (egg-laying organ) for piercing the stems of the plant. The eggs hatch within a few days, and long thin larvae emerge from the stem to crawl about the pond. These larvae grow quickly and can reach a length of 6 centimetres. They look rather like long-legged earwigs and are very ferocious, capable of overpowering tadpoles and small fish, although smaller invertebrates make up most of their diet.

Where would you find a tadpole up a tree?

In the rainforests of Amazonia. Here there are plants called bromeliads growing high up on the branches of trees. The leaves of bromeliads form a watertight bowl, in which rainwater can collect. The water is there for the plant's benefit, but it also forms a miniature pond-in-the-sky which is used by dragonflies and mosquitoes for laying their eggs. Some frogs raise their tadpoles here, and many other small animals live and breed in the water, high above the forest floor.

Why does a hippopotamus have its eyes on top of its head?

So that it can walk or wallow in water with most of its head submerged. Its nostrils are also placed high up on its snout, so it can breathe when doing this – only its eyes, ears and nostrils stick out of the water. Hippos need to stay almost completely submerged in water during the daytime because their thin skin rapidly loses moisture in the sun.

Which waterbird carries its young on its back?

The Great Crested Grebe is best known for this. The chicks nestle between its wings and the grebe swims away with them 'on board'. By doing this both the mother grebe and chicks can escape from danger more quickly. Otherwise the slow-swimming chicks would make an easy target for any predator.

The Black Heron spreads its wings to darken the surface of the water when fishing.

Which bird shades the water with its wings when hunting?

The Black Heron of Africa. It lowers its head and fans out both wings so that they cast an almost-circular shadow. It is possible that fish are attracted to the shady water, or it may just make passing fish easier to see.

What do Everglade Kites eat?

The Everglade Kite is a fussy eater: it will eat nothing but *Pomacea* water snails. The elongated upper half of its beak is specially adapted for prising the snails out of their shells, which it does with great dexterity while standing on one foot.

Which birds make a call like a ship's foghorn?

The bitterns are secretive birds of marshland and like tall reeds and other vegetation where they can hide. Their booming call is heard often in such places, but the birds themselves are rarely seen. Before the breeding season the airway leading to the male's lungs becomes larger and more elastic, so that it can be inflated when he booms. This is what makes the sound so loud and resonant. It can sometimes be heard up to 5 kilometres away.

Which animals steal oxygen from plants?

The larvae of some flies spend their early lives in ponds, and get oxygen by piercing the leaves of pondweed. Using a sharp siphon, the fly larva can take the oxygen it needs from the plant's air spaces.

What do pondskaters and backswimmers have in common?

They are both the insect equivalent of vultures. They feed on other insects that have accidentally fallen into their pond and drowned. These tiny corpses float on the surface of the water where the pondskaters and backswimmers suck out their body juices with piercing mouthparts. The difference between them is that pondskaters live above water, while backswimmers live below, rowing themselves along with two powerful legs. There is fierce competition between them for food, and the more aggressive backswimmers usually win any tussle. When their food supply runs out, both insects can take to the air and fly to a new pond.

Which pond creatures breathe through 'snorkels'?

Breathing through small tubes which stick out above the water is one way in which pond creatures such as mosquito larvae, dronefly larvae and Water Scorpions are assured of their oxygen supply.

Which bird is also known as a 'snake bird'?

The Anhinga of Central and South America, Africa and Asia is also known as 'snake bird' because of its long, snake-like neck. An underwater diver, it shoots its neck out to spear fish with its dagger-like beak. As it swims along the water surface, it often keeps all but its head and neck below the water, emphasizing its snake-like appearance.

What are ducks doing when you just see their tails sticking up out of the water?

Eating water weed growing on the bottom. The ducks are said to be 'upending'. Not all ducks do this, because different ducks eat different things.

The Shelduck searching for food on the river bed.

Why is the Whirligig Beetle so called?

Because it spins round on the surface of ponds in dizzying circles. No one is sure why this little beetle behaves in such an odd way. It has been suggested that the ripples it sets up act in the same way as sound waves for an echolocating bat: that the beetle detects them as they are reflected from objects around it. This seems unlikely because whirligig beetles usually whirl about in groups, so there would be a confusing number of different ripples. From watching whirligigs, some naturalists conclude that they whirl to escape predators or deter them from launching an attack.

Which moth spends its whole life underwater?

The female Water Moth. This wingless moth swims about underwater and only comes to the surface to mate. The male, which looks like a normal moth, flies down to the water surface to find her. Sometimes the male plucks the female from the water and carries her through the air for a while as they mate, but usually they mate on the water's surface. The female lays her eggs on water plants. Sometimes these eggs hatch into winged females, which fly off to colonize new ponds and lakes.

Do Dancing Cranes really dance?

Yes, but so do all cranes. Their dances are mainly seen in the breeding season, and help the male and female to prepare themselves for nesting. The two cranes bow to each other, dance, leap and run about wildly. Because most cranes nest in remote, marshy areas, few people see these spectacular displays.

Crane

Unusual Habitats

Which animal lives on pools of oil?

A small fly which is found in parts of North America where crude oil bubbles up out of the ground. The fly preys on other insects that accidentally fall into the oil and cannot escape.

Which animals bore into solid rock?

Several different kinds of shelled molluscs do this, including the piddocks, the gapers, the rock borers and the date mussels. These shellfish have sharp, rasping edges to their shells. By moving them back and forwards with a sawing action, the mollusc can slowly bore its way into soft rock such as chalk or sandstone.

Which animals depend on the heat of the Earth's core for their food?

The animals that live around hydrothermal vents in the depths of the ocean. These vents are places where the molten core of the Earth is very near the surface. Seawater filters down, is heated, then shoots up through the vent. As well as being extremely hot, the water is now rich in dissolved minerals, and there are certain bacteria that can use the energy in these minerals to make food. All the other animals around the vent, such as giant beardworms, clams and blind crabs, are ultimately dependent on these bacteria for their food.

Which animals make their own habitat, where they control the temperature and grow their own food?

The termites known as *Macrotermes bellicosus*. These tiny insects live in colonies numbering several million. They build towering mounds of mud up to six metres high inside which they nest. There are special ventilation shafts which control the temperature of the nest, and even the amount of moisture in the air.

Which fish are completely blind?

Cave-dwelling fish, such as the Cave Characin. These fish live in subterranean pools where there is no light at all. To compensate for their lack of vision, they have other well-developed senses, including a form of echolocation, like that of bats. Their own movements produce vibrations in the surrounding water, and these are reflected from objects near them. The Cave Characin can pick up such reflections and use them to detect its prey.

Do booklice really live in books?

Yes. These tiny insects feed on the glue used to bind the pages of a book. Many modern glues are not edible, but booklice are not fussy eaters. They can also live on tiny crumbs of food dropped on tables and carpets, and can hide in any crevice about the house.

Which monkey uses hot springs to keep warm?

The Japanese Macaque, the most northerly monkey in the world, and one of the few to see snow. These macaques have a much thicker coat of fur than other monkeys, but still suffer from the near-freezing temperatures in winter. By immersing themselves up to the neck in thermal pools (where warm water wells up from close to the Earth's hot core) they survive the coldest days.

What is a kopje and what kind of animals live on one?

A kopje is an 'island of rock' found on the savan-nahs of Africa. These islands of smooth, fissured granite are large enough to support their own communities of animals. Up to 30 metres high, the kopje has its own bushes and trees which feed insects, dik-diks (small antelope), troops of baboons and an unusual mammal, the Rock Hyrax. Lizards feed on the insects, and various birds of prey swoop down upon the Rock Hyraxes. One hawk has excep-tionally long legs which it uses for prising small animals out of the cracks in the rock. Lying on its side, with its wings back and legs fully extended, the hawk can reach into a narrow crevice and grab a cowering lizard with its claws.

Kopjes on the African savannah.

Which birds can 'see in the dark', using echolocation like that of bats?

Birds that nest in caves. The main ones to do this are the Oilbird of the Caribbean and South America, and the Cave-nesting Swiftlets of south-east Asia. The Oilbird is an unusual species, the only noc-turnal fruit-eater in the bird world. Cave-nesting Swiftlets feed on insects. Both echolocate using audible clicks, rather than the ultrasonic sounds of bats. By nesting in caves they escape from most predators.

Which animals spend their whole adult lives attached to a whale, but are not parasites?

Barnacles. They favour the Right Whales and Hump-back Whales, which have knobbly outgrowths on their heads. These become infested with parasites as well as clumps of barnacles, but they do not seem to cause the whales any discomfort. Why the whales have these outgrowths is not known. For the Bar-nacles a whale is just as good a surface for attach-ment as a rock. Today, whale barnacles are often found attached to the very large ships that carry crude oil, suggesting that the whale does not offer them much apart from a platform to feed on.

Japanese Macaques bathe in hot springs to keep warm during winter.

ANIMALS IN DANGER

Where are the most extinctions occurring at present?

In the tropical rainforests. This is because the number of species in tropical forests is exceptionally high, and they are now being destroyed very rapidly. The majority of animals becoming extinct are insects and other invertebrates, many of which have probably never been studied or given a name. Larger animals, such as birds and mammals, are also threatened. The rainforests are shrinking day by day as they are cleared for agriculture and for the timber, and some Amazon tribes are also losing their homes.

As the tropical rainforests are cleared for timber and grazing many species that live there are becoming extinct.

Why is the Indus Dolphin endangered?

Because the Indus River has been extensively dammed, dividing it up into ten separate sections. This prevents both fish and dolphins moving up and down the river, and reduces the amount of food available as a result. Large animals such as dolphins need to be able to move on when they exhaust the food supply in one area. The dolphins are also hunted, and this has helped to reduce their numbers to less than 600.

Which bird was saved from extinction by moving the entire population?

The Chatham Island Black Robin, which occurred only on four small islands off New Zealand. It died out on three, and by 1976 there were only seven birds left on the fourth island. The habitat there was being damaged, so all the birds were moved to another island with a better habitat. The species is still endangered, but the total population now numbers over 20.

What is (or was) a babirusa?

A type of wild pig, with four unusual tusks. One pair of tusks grows vertically upwards through the muzzle, in front of the eyes. Babirusas are found only in Sulawesi, an island in south-east Asia, and live in forested areas near lakes and rivers. Hunting babirusas to supply city restaurants may have brought them close to extinction. It is hard to be sure how many are left, because the babirusa is a secretive and elusive animal.

Which insects, apart from butterflies, are most in danger at present?

The dragonflies. Their young develop underwater, so they are threatened by the widespread drainage of ponds, lakes and marshes. Pesticides flowing into the water from farmland are also a problem, as dragonfly larvae need clean, unpolluted water.

Which extinct bird was once so numerous its flocks could darken the sky?

The Passenger Pigeon of North America. This nomadic bird moved about in enormous flocks, estimated at up to 2000 million birds in size. The flocks were up to six kilometres wide and 475 kilometres long, and took several days to pass by, during which time they darkened the sky and created a chill wind below them with their rapid flight. Intensive hunting by European settlers eventually took its toll. The effects of hunting were made worse by the destruction of forests, which reduced the supply of acorns and beechnuts for the huge flocks to feed on. Within 300 years the Passenger Pigeon was extinct in the wild. No wild birds were seen after 1889 and the last captive bird died in Cincinnati Zoo in 1914.

Which deer survives only in captivity?

Père David's deer, whose marshy homelands in China have all been drained for rice-growing.

Which was the first animal to be reintroduced, after becoming extinct in the wild?

The Arabian Oryx. Its dramatic decline was due to uncontrolled hunting. The arrival of motor vehicles and guns increased the level of destruction, and by the early 1960s there were only about 100–200 animals left. In 1962 three of these oryx were captured and combined with zoo animals to form a captive breeding herd. In 1972 the last wild oryx were shot. By the 1980s, there were enough captive-bred oryx to reintroduce a herd. At first, they were kept within a fenced area, but eventually allowed to roam freely. There is now a complete ban on hunting in most countries where the oryx occurs.

How can fishing harm swans?

By poisoning them with lead. Fishermen need weights for their lines, and lead is traditionally used. But when the weights are lost or thrown away, they sink to the bottom. Swans, like so many birds, pick up grit which they use to grind up their food. If a swan picks up a lead weight with its grit, that lead will stay inside its body and slowly poison it. There are alternatives to lead which are non-toxic, but it has been difficult to persuade some fishermen to use these.

Swan

Why did the peregrine die out in eastern North America in the 1960s?

Because of the widespread use of the insecticide, DDT. This insecticide affects birds badly because it makes them lay thin-shelled eggs. When the birds sit on the eggs in the nest, they break under their weight. Birds of prey are more badly affected than others, and the peregrine was not the only one to go into a sharp decline. The same effect was seen in other parts of the world as well.

The Arabian Oryx: saved from extinction

127

A dolphin with its young

Why is tuna fishing a threat to dolphins?

Because some types of dolphin like to swim with shoals of tuna. Off the western coast of North America, fishermen use the dolphins to locate the tuna, which are usually swimming below them, out of sight. When the tuna are netted, the dolphins are also killed.

Which 'extinct' bird was discovered alive in 1948?

The Takahe of New Zealand, a beautiful relative of the coots and moorhens, with glossy blue and green plumage and a large crimson beak. This flightless bird lives in remote valleys, high up in the mountains of New Zealand. After not being seen for many years, it was found again in 1948. However, there are only about 100 pairs, which means that the bird is endangered. Its future is now brighter, however, thanks to a successful breeding programme.

Where do the pieces of coral sold as souvenirs and ornaments come from?

From living coral reefs. These are either blown up with dynamite or broken up with iron bars dragged by ships. This shatters the coral into pieces that can be sold. Either process is very destructive. A reef takes thousands of years to build up, and provides a home for thousands of different animals.

Why is there concern about the Koala?

Because so much native eucalyptus forest is being destroyed in Australia. If food is plentiful, koalas are great survivors. They managed to recover from intensive hunting between 1900 and 1930, and were, until relatively recently, expanding in most areas. But the accelerating pace of forest destruction is a threat to them, as to many other Australian animals.

The Koala's habitat is shrinking year by year.

Why are so many endangered species found on remote islands?

Because island animals have evolved in an isolated situation, often with few predators and little competition from other species. They may have become unable to defend themselves and their young. Or they may be unable to escape from predators, as with many flightless birds. They survived perfectly well until people arrived on the island, bringing dogs, cats and rats. Goats, pigs and donkeys are problems because they damage the vegetation leaving less for the native animals.

Large Copper

Which was the first butterfly to be reintroduced in the wild?

The Large Copper, which was reintroduced into Britain in 1898, using butterflies from Europe. The butterfly had originally died out due to drainage of the fens and over-enthusiastic collecting by Victorian naturalists. This first reintroduction was unsuccessful, but in 1927 a second attempt was made, and these butterflies survived.

How did Right Whales get their name?

They were given this name by the early whalers, who considered them the 'right' whales to kill, because they were slow enough to be caught by sailing ships, or even rowing boats. Thanks to their lack of technology, these old-time whalers did not succeed in wiping out any species of Right Whale. But all three species were reduced to dangerously low levels. Despite many years of protection, their numbers are still very small, and two of the three are classed as endangered.

Right Whale

Which animal is endangered by our liking for perfume?

The Musk Deer of the Himalayas. Its scent gland provides musk, which is highly valued as a stabiliser for perfumes. Even in areas where it is protected, the Musk Deer is still killed by poachers.

Will the 'greenhouse effect' mean that more species are endangered?

Yes, although its precise effects cannot be predicted at the moment. We know there will be a rise in sea level and this will submerge some islands, such as the Maldives, completely. It will also cover up many coastal sites that are important for birds and other animals, so reducing their food supply. The general warming will increase the spread of deserts into scrub and savannah areas and this will pose a threat to some species. Changes in climate often occurred in prehistoric times and we know from fossils that some species became extinct. The effect today is likely to be far more damaging, because many habitats have already been destroyed and populations of wild animals are already reduced in size. This makes it less likely that species can evolve to meet the challenges of a climatic change.

Which bird breeds successfully in captivity but not in the wild?

The Hawaiian Goose, or Nene. There were once about 25,000 of these geese on Hawaii, but the introduction of alien animals proved fatal for them. Their numbers were reduced to about 30 by the early 1950s. From 13 birds already in captivity, a breeding programme was started. This was so successful that there are over 1300 Nenes in captivity today. Another 2000 have been released on Hawaii, but they have failed to establish themselves there, because many of the original problems still exist.

Which animals are being killed to make dagger handles?

The rhinoceroses, especially the African species. Their horns are valued in the Middle East for making the handles of ceremonial daggers. All species of rhinoceros are now dangerously low in numbers.

Rhinoceros

How is the Black Rhinoceros being protected from poachers?

By the removal of its horns. In some national parks in Africa, wardens are immobilizing the rhinoceroses with tranquilizing darts, then sawing off their horns. This operation apparently does the rhinos no lasting damage, but it takes away all their value to poachers.

Why does the fashion for crocodile skin endanger turtles?

The killing of crocodiles for their skins has reduced their numbers all over the world. In some countries they are now kept on special farms, but the demand for crocodile skin still exceeds supply. Turtle skin is used as a substitute, and thousands of turtles are killed every year, as they come ashore to lay their eggs.

What is Abbot's Booby, and why is it endangered?

Abbot's Booby is a seabird which nests in only one place in the world, on Christmas Island in the Indian Ocean. This island has valuable deposits of phosphates, which can be used as fertilizer. If mining for phosphates is allowed to go ahead, it will mean extinction for Abbot's Booby.

When is the African Elephant expected to become extinct?

At present rates of hunting, it will die out in about 1995. Most hunting is illegal, the elephants being killed for their tusks, which provide ivory. Ivory is used only for decorative objects and piano keys. The search is on for a man-made substitute.

Thousands of African Elephants are killed every year for their ivory tusks.

What is Europe's rarest breeding bird?

The Gadfly Petrel, or Freira, found only on the island of Madeira. There are no more than 20 pairs of this seabird left. Black rats are the main problem, because they eat both eggs and chicks. The only hope for the Freira is to wipe out the rats on the cliff ledges where the birds breed. This is currently being attempted, but it is difficult work.

Blue Whale: it is now illegal to hunt them.

Why is the Giant Panda so rare?

This panda was probably never common, and it is entirely dependent on bamboo for food. It needs enormous amounts of bamboo so each panda has a very large territory. As the bamboo groves have been cut down to make way for agriculture, the panda's habitat has been slowly disappearing. Even where the bamboo remains, it is often in such small areas that only two or three pandas can live there. They will not cross open country, so they cannot reach other groups of pandas to find a mate. Small isolated groups of this kind soon die out.

How many Blue Whales are there left?

About 1000. For a large animal like the Blue Whale, which breeds only slowly, this is a dangerously low number. Blue Whales have been completely protected since 1967, but there has been no marked increase in numbers, and the species is still endangered.

What is the rarest Australian mammal?

Is is probably the Rabbit Bandicoot, an unusual marsupial with very long ears and a sharply pointed snout. It lives in dry woodland and scrub, and digs in the ground for beetle grubs and termites, poking its long nose into the holes to find its prey. The Rabbit Bandicoot, also known as the Greater Bilby, has declined due to grazing by cattle, sheep and rabbits. A closely related species, the Lesser Rabbit Bandicoot, died out earlier this century.

What kind of animal is the Tasmanian Tiger?

Not a tiger, but a marsupial mammal. It is more closely related to kangaroos and koalas than to the tigers of India. The first Europeans to reach Australia called it a 'tiger' because of the striped pattern on its hindquarters. The Tasmanian Tiger – or Thylacine, as it is often known – is thought to be extinct. But there are occasional reports of some animals still living in remote parts of Tasmania. It once inhabited the whole of Australia.

Tasmanian Tiger

What is the greatest threat to the European Puffin?

Large-scale fishing for sand-eels, tiny fish which the puffins (and many other seabirds) use for food. Sand-eels are especially important in the breeding season, for feeding the growing chicks. In recent years large numbers of sand-eels have been caught and the numbers have declined dramatically. Many puffins have failed to breed, and many chicks starve.

Otters are poisoned by farmers' pesticides.

Which animal was safe until its nesting site was discovered?

Kemp's Ridley Turtle. Although common in the Gulf of Mexico, no one knew where it went to lay its eggs. A biologist with a fascination for turtles spent many years trying to find its breeding beach, and finally succeeded in 1947. He discovered that all the turtles of this species came to the same deserted spot on the Mexican coast. There were as many as 40,000 female turtles on this beach every year. As news of the find spread, fishermen moved in, and within 30 years, there were very few of these turtles left. The species is now considered to be endangered.

Why are birds of prey and otters so badly affected by the pesticides that farmers use?

Because many pesticides are not broken down by the body, but are stored in the fat. When an insect or tadpole is eaten by a small fish, that fish acquires all the pesticide its prey had eaten in its lifetime. The small fish may be eaten by larger fish and the next fish up the 'food chain' gets an even larger dose, and this fish may then be eaten by an otter or bird of prey. These 'top predators' accumulate a huge dose of pesticide in this way, and sometimes suffer severe poisoning as a result.

Where does the Giant Earwig live?

On the island of St Helena. The Giant Earwig measures up to 7.8 centimetres and is becoming increasingly rare. Rats and Giant Centipedes, both introduced by humans, have killed a great many. There is now a captive breeding programme at London Zoo, aimed at reintroducing the earwig.

Where was the Javan Rhino rediscovered in 1988?

In southern Vietnam. This is good news, because there are only about 50 left on Java itself, and there are none anywhere else. The population found in Vietnam probably numbers about 10–15. It will be many years before it is safe.

Why is the North American Whooping Crane endangered?

Because so many have been shot by hunters as they migrate between their breeding grounds and the places where they spend the winter.

What was the 'penguin of the north' and when did it become extinct?

The Great Auk, a large flightless bird found only in the North Atlantic. Although unrelated to the penguins, it was flightless and looked quite penguin-like. This was a result of adapting to the same way of life, in which flying was abandoned in favour of high-speed swimming. This unique and fascinating bird was wiped out by ruthless hunting for meat and feathers. The last Great Auks died out in the mid-19th century.

What is being done to curb the trade in endangered wild animals?

About 90 countries have signed the Convention on Trade in Endangered Species (CITES, for short) which prohibits the export of endangered plants and animals. However, enforcement of this treaty is difficult, and many countries have yet to sign.

Beavers build dams in which to live.

What is a Kakapo?

A flightless parrot from New Zealand. It is the largest parrot in the world, and the only flightless species. A nocturnal ground-dweller, its chicks are vulnerable to attack by rats, which first arrived with the Maoris. The future of this parrot depends on efforts to establish it on small islands, where there are no introduced predators.

What is the greatest worldwide threat to animals?

The destruction of their habitats – the forests, prairies, coral reefs, swamps or other places in which they live. Most of the animals that die out in the coming century will do so because we have destroyed their homes. To reduce the damage, we need to find ways of exploiting natural resources less destructively, and restricting the growth of human populations.

Which large rodent has been reintroduced into France and Austria?

The beaver, once found throughout Europe, but now restricted to parts of Scandinavia, Finland, Poland and Germany.

WHO?

Who discovered the Giant Panda?

The French missionary Père Armand David is credited with the discovery of the Giant Panda in 1869, although he did not see an acutal live panda. His 'discovery' was of a few furs of an unusual two-toned bear.

Who proposed the theory of evolution?

Charles Darwin (1809–82) first thought of the theory of evolution by natural selection in about 1840, but he didn't publish it until 1858.

Who nearly pipped Darwin to the post?

Darwin spent nearly 20 years collecting evidence for his theory of evolution, but it wasn't until he received a letter from another English naturalist, Alfred Russel Wallace (1823–1913), that he was prompted into action. Wallace thought of the same theory quite independently, but he was quite happy for Darwin to receive all the praise.

Who was opposed to Darwin's theory of evolution?

Many Christians were at first bitterly opposed to Darwin's theory, for it conflicted with the Bible's account of how all life had come into being. According to the Bible, the world and all living things were created by God in six days in the year 4004BC.

Who was Linnaeus?

Carolus Linnaeus (1707–78) (Carl von Linné) devised the system of naming plants and animals which we use today. He gave every living thing two Latin names, the first name being the group or *genus* name, and the second the *species* name.

Who wrote the first animal encyclopedia?

The Greek philosopher Aristotle (384–322BC) compiled the first animal encyclopedia, *Historia Animalium*, in 335BC. In it he described over 300 species of vertebrates with reasonable accuracy.

Who discovered penicillin?

Sir Alexander Fleming (1881–1955) stumbled across penicillin in one of the round dishes in which he was growing harmful bacteria. A spore (seed) of a mould called *Penicillium* landed in the dish and killed off the harmful bacteria.

Who was Rikki Tikki Tavi?

Rikki Tikki Tavi was the central character in a book by Rudyard Kipling. He was an Indian mongoose who was kept as a pet by an English family while staying in India. He was given his name because of his incessant chattering.

Who was Gregor Mendel?

Gregor Mendel (1822–84) was an Austrian monk whose important work on pea plants led to the formulation of the laws of heredity (or the ways in which offspring inherit the characteristics of their parents).

Who spent three days inside a whale?

Jonah, a prophet of the Old Testament is supposed to have spent three days inside a whale. He was thrown overboard during a storm at sea for refusing to obey God's command, and when he was safely ashore, he devoted the rest of his life to serving God.

Who was Moby Dick?

Moby Dick was a white whale in Herman Melville's novel of the same name. This gripping story tells of the long battle between an old whaling captain (Captain Ahab) and an aggressive white whale.

Who wrote the *Natural History of Selborne*?

Gilbert White (1720–93) was the first English naturalist to write about his observations of nature in a clear and detailed way. His collection of essays about the countryside surrounding his home village of Selborne in Hampshire was published as a book in 1788.

WHAT?

What is the biggest threat to wildlife?

Humans pose the biggest threat to wildlife. By destroying the areas where they live, by overhunting them for their fur and flesh and by introducing domestic livestock into their natural habitats, they threaten the existence of scores of wild animals.

What is ambergris?

Ambergris is a waxy substance found in the intestine of the Sperm Whale. It is used in making perfume.

What is the world's fastest-moving living creature?

The Peregrine Falcon has been known to achieve speeds of 350 kilometres per hour when diving at an angle of 45 degrees.

Which mammal uses a furry cape to fly?

The colugo of the south-east Asian rainforests is one of the most efficient of the gliding mammals and is capable of gliding over a hundred metres through its forest home. So well adapted is the colugo to a life in the trees, that it is unable to walk properly on the ground.

What do Crabeater Seals eat?

Crabeater Seals do not eat crabs. Their diet consists largely of krill, which they strain from the waters of the Antarctic by means of their intricately notched teeth.

What is unusual about an aye-aye's fingers?

The aye-aye of Madagascar is a primitive primate which eats beetle larvae. The third finger on its hand is particularly long and bony, and it uses this finger to probe into holes in trees and extract any larvae within. Unusually for a primate, the aye-aye has claws rather than fingernails.

Which insect lays eggs on stalks?

The eggs of the delicate lacewing are attached to leaves and twigs by long, hair-like stalks to protect them from predators.

Which insect is the swiftest-flying?

The dragonfly is among the fastest of all insects – in fact, they are so swift and active that apart from the hobby, a small bird of prey, they have few natural predators.

What is a badger's home called?

Badgers are natural diggers with immensely strong legs. They live in a large system of underground burrows known as a *set*.

Which animal has the finest wool?

The graceful vicuna of the Andes Mountains in South America is thought to have the finest quality wool. It needs its thick woolly coat to withstand the freezing temperatures of its mountain home.

What is a thylacine?

A thylacine, or 'Tasmanian tiger', is the largest flesh-eating marsupial known. It looks rather like a stripy wolf, and it is thought to prey on wallabies, bandicoots and birds. Sadly, this animal has probably been hunted to extinction by sheep and poultry farmers.

What is an okapi?

An okapi is a curious-looking creature of the African rainforest, with striped hindlegs and two short skin-covered horns on its head. At first, scientists thought that it was related to the zebra, but in fact it bears closer resemblance to the ancestors of the giraffe.

What is a Pea Crab?

A Pea Crab is a small, round, soft-bodied crab which lives in the shells of mussels. They take their food from their host's supply, and sometimes take a nibble from the mussel's gills. It is thought that Pea Crabs warn their hosts of approaching danger.

What do elephants use their trunks for?

An elephant's trunk is amazingly strong and muscular, allowing it to pull branches from trees or to pull up saplings by the roots. It is also very sensitive, and can pick up a single peanut from the ground. It also has its uses as a hose and as an extra hand for keeping baby elephants in line.

Which bird is known to hibernate?

The Common Poorwill of North America and Mexico is the only bird known to hibernate. Each year it will seek out the same rock crevice (or similar sheltered place) and fall into a state of torpor, allowing its body temperature and heartbeat to drop to minimal levels.

What is an elver?

An elver is a young eel. The European eel breeds in the Sargasso Sea, and the larvae swim to Europe, taking three years to complete the journey. By the time they enter the river estuaries they have developed into elvers.

What colour is a ptarmigan?

The colour of a ptarmigan's plumage depends on the time of year: in summer it is a mottled brown to blend in with the forest background, while in the winter it changes to white, for greater protection in the winter snows.

What does an armadillo do when danger threatens?

Armadillos are equipped with a bony armour, which provides excellent protection when the animal is threatened. Some species are able to roll themselves up into a ball to protect their limbs and soft bellies.

What do Cookiecutter Sharks eat?

Cookiecutter Sharks rarely grow bigger than 50 centimetres – and yet their diet consists of neat chunks taken out of fish much larger than themselves. Whales, dolphins and all big fish are fair game to this intrepid shark, whose mouth fixes on to its host like a suction pad. Once in place, it drives its razor-sharp teeth into the bigger fish's flesh.

What do pandas eat?

Pandas are fussy eaters, whose diet consists almost exclusively of bamboo. Because of the relatively unnutritious content of its food, it has to spend over ten hours a day feeding.

What animals did sailors used to mistake for mermaids?

After a long spell at sea, it is quite likely that the 'mermaids' that sailors used to report seeing were none other than the harmless dugongs of the Indian Ocean. These aquatic mammals are shy, solitary creatures and bear no resemblance to the female human.

What is cuckoo spit made of?

Cuckoo spit is the protective foam made by the larva of the froghopper insect. This froth both hides the larva and prevents it from drying out.

What does the White-eared Hummingbird use to make its nest?

The White-eared Hummingbird builds an amazingly delicate cup-shaped nest which, apart from the mossy base, is composed largely of spiders' webs.

What are rhinoceros horns made of?

For a long time it was thought that the horns of rhinoceroses were made of densely matted hair, but in fact they consist of tough fibres which grow up from the skin. They are not connected to the skull so are not 'true' horns like the horns of an antelope.

What is a zorilla's best mode of defence?

A zorilla is one of the smelliest animals known. When threatened, it brandishes its bushy white tail before squirting an acrid-smelling substance from its anal glands.

What is grocer's itch?

Grocer's itch is an irritation of the skin caused by contact with mites which feed on stored foodstuffs, such as flour, sugar and dried fruit.

What do springboks do if they sense danger?

When alarmed, springboks will perform a number of stiff-legged jumps in the air, sometimes bounding as high as three and a half metres. This peculiar bouncing behaviour is called *pronking*.

Which bird is supposed to bring luck to warriors?

Muslim warriors have long held the belief that if a Brahminy Kite flies over them then they will be victorious in battle.

What is unusual about the sleeping arrangements of the bananaquit?

The bananaquit is a small, tropical bird common in forests, gardens and open country. It builds a spherical nest specifically for sleeping in – and males and females each have separate nests.

Which lizard squirts blood?

When alarmed, the Horned Toad of North America (which in fact is a lizard) is believed to squirt blood from its eyes at its assailant, although no-one knows how it manages to do this.

What is a matamata?

A matamata is a strange-looking turtle found in the rivers of northern South America. Its shell is rough and lumpy and its head, which is supported by a long, snake-like neck, is flat and almost triangular in shape. The turtle is so well camouflaged on the river bottom that it simply waits for unsuspecting fish to swim by before opening its huge mouth and sucking them in.

Which snake likes to eat bats?

The Cuban Tree Boa lurks around the entrances to caves in Cuba where bats are known to roost, and lunges at the bats as they fly in and out. Usually the snakes are fairly adept at catching the bats, although how they manage to locate them in the dark is still something of a mystery.

What fish can live in hot water?

At the southern end of Death Valley, Nevada, USA, there is a series of small streams and lakes. These are the home of desert pupfish that survive in water temperatures of over 38°C.

Which bird is also known as a windhover?

Windhover is an old folk name for the kestrel. It arose no doubt because of the seemingly effortless way the kestrel hovers in mid-air as it scans the ground below for prey.

What is the response of a Bearded Dragon to danger?

The Bearded Dragon of the Australian outback is a formidable-looking lizard whose body is covered in small spines. Under its chin is a spiny throat pouch which can be erected when alarmed. The lizard will hold its ground, open its yellow mouth, puff out its beard and hiss menacingly at its attacker.

What action does a Bombardier Beetle take to deter a predator?

Bombardier Beetles have a most astonishing defence mechanism. When threatened, they are able to eject a boiling hot corrosive liquid from their rear end – enough to deter the most persistent predator.

What special relationship do Tick-birds have with rhinoceroses?

Tick-birds live off the numerous ticks and insects which are attached to the rhinoceros's body, while the short-sighted rhinoceros gains not only a cleaning service, but also an alarm system, as the bird will utter warning cries if danger threatens.

What are pheromones?

Pheromones are chemical substances released by an animal which affect the behaviour or development of other animals of the same species. Pheromones may be secreted in urine, dung or from special glands. Bees and ants are examples of insects which rely on pheromones to communicate.

137

What distinguishes a Conger Eel from freshwater eels?

Conger eels are thick-bodied marine eels, growing up to three metres in length. Their bodies have no scales, unlike those of freshwater eels.

What do Brazilian Tree Frogs build their nests with?

Brazilian Tree Frogs use clay to build their crater-shaped nests in shallow water. Fashioning the walls to a height of ten centimetres with the skill of an artisan, the frogs' nests (which are about 30 centimetres across) form an effective barrier between the eggs and any predatory fish.

What are Colorado Beetles?

Colorado Beetles are notorious pests of potato crops. Originally the insect used to feed on buffalo burr, which belongs to the same family as the potato. Unfortunately the leaves of potato and buffalo burr have a similar taste.

Which butterfly does the African Swallowtail mimick?

The normal form of the African Swallowtail Butterfly is the male form: a cream-colour with dark 'tailed' wings. The female may sometimes be quite unlike the male, as she frequently mimicks the colouring and wing pattern of the inedible butterflies of the milkweed family (which are predominantly orange and black). In this way she runs less risk of being eaten by predators.

What is a doodlebug?

A doodlebug is the larva of an Ant-lion which, when fully grown, resembles a small dragonfly. The doodlebug digs a cone-shaped pit in loose sandy soil and then waits for insects – particularly ants – to fall into it. It then seizes them and sucks them dry.

Which fish gives us caviare?

Caviare is made from the eggs of the sturgeon fish. Unfortunately pollution and overfishing have combined to make this fish extremely rare (and caviare very expensive).

What is a wobbegong?

A wobbegong is a Carpet Shark which rests on the sea bed looking like a rock covered in sea weed. It is distinguished from other sharks by a fringe of fleshy lobes around its head which look like seaweed.

What sort of creature is a tapir?

A tapir is a sturdy animal with stocky legs and a short, movable trunk. Its body is covered in bristly hair, and it has four toes on its front feet and three on its hind. Tapirs are shy, nocturnal animals which live in the rainforests of Brazil and south-east Asia.

What does a hornbill use its beak for?

Hornbills are tropical birds with enormous beaks bearing horny projections. The oddly shaped beaks are used for nesting, passing food through holes in trees and courtship displays.

Which insect was used to control the spread of Prickly Pear in Australia?

The Prickly Pear Cactus was introduced to Australia at the end of the 18th century, and within a hundred years it had spread over such a wide area that it was regarded as a pest. A small moth from Argentina, *Cactoblastis*, whose larvae burrow into the flesh of the prickly pear, was imported to control its spread.

What is a narwhal?

A narwhal is a white whale with an extraordinary spiral tusk growing from its snout. In fact this tusk is its upper left incisor and grows to a length of nearly three metres.

Which is the smallest flesh-eating mammal?

The Least Weasel, a predator of mice and small mammals, is the world's smallest carnivorous mammal.

What is a quoll?

A quoll is a cat-sized, predatory marsupial from south-east Australia. It hunts mainly at night, preying on rats, mice, birds and insects.

What do Polar Bears eat?

Polar Bears are huge white bears of the Arctic north. Their diet consists of seals, fish, Arctic hares, seabirds and even reindeer. Their diet is supplemented in the summer with the leaves and berries of tundra plants.

What do Sea Otters do before they go to sleep?

Sea Otters sleep floating in the water, but before nodding off they wrap strands of kelp seaweed around their bodies to prevent them from drifting in the current.

What is the difference between a Marsupial Mole and a European Mole?

Apart from the differences in how they develop, Marsupial Moles and European Moles have a lot in common. Both are efficient underground burrowers, although the burrows of the Marsupial Mole tend to be less permanent than those of the European Mole. A Marsupial Mole is easily recognized by its paler coat and horny nose shield.

What do ground-nesting birds do to lure predators away from their nests?

It is not uncommon for a ground-nesting bird to feign injury to attract a predator away from her nest. The killdeer of North America, for example, will pretend to have a broken wing in order to distract a potential attacker.

What do paperwasps use to make their nests?

Paperwasps build their nests using woodshavings which they chew into a pulp with their saliva to make paper. The lightness of their building material enables them to construct large nests.

What sort of nest does a wren build?

A wren's nest is a cosy spherical structure with a small side opening, which is often well hidden in the hedgerow or undergrowth. The wren builds its nest from plant material taken from the immediate area, so that it blends in well with the background.

What does MacGregor's Bowerbird build?

Distinguished by a bright orange crest on an otherwise dull plumage, the male MacGregor's Bowerbird busies himself building a saucer-shaped platform of moss underneath a central column of twigs. The male decorates his bower with colourful objects in the hope of attracting a passing female.

Which way does the fur on a sloth grow?

A sloth spends almost the whole of its life asleep in the trees, hanging upside down from the branches. Because of the way it hangs, its hair grows 'backwards', from its stomach towards its back.

What is a fossil?

A fossil is a naturally formed replica, or copy, of a living plant or animal, preserved in rock. It usually shows just the hard parts of the living thing, such as the bones, shell or teeth. Only if the rock has a very fine structure will it show the soft parts of the body, such as the skin or feathers.

What were the first animals to live on Earth like?

They were soft-bodied creatures like worms and jellyfish. Scientists have found fossils of these animals in fine-grained rocks in Australia. Before these creatures lived there were even smaller living things, consisting of just one cell. The very first living things were probably like bacteria, which are tiny single cells, with a very simple structure.

What is the title of Darwin's most famous book?

On the Origin of Species by means of Natural Selection, or the Preservation of Favoured Races in the Struggle for Life. Fortunately this was soon shortened to *The Origin of Species.*

What was the largest flying animal ever to have lived?

A pterosaur called *Quetzalcoatlus*, whose remains were found in Texas in 1972. This airborne giant had a wingspan of 15 metres, which is as large as a light aeroplane.

What is the theory evolution?

Evolution is a process of very slow, gradual changes that happens to all living things. It is so slow that we cannot see it happening around us. But we can tell that it has happened by looking at fossils. If you look at the fossils of horses from about 40 million years ago, they were only about half the size of horses today. Horses have gradually evolved into larger animals, each generation being a fraction larger than the one before. This happens as a result of 'natural selection'.

What is the difference between a snake and an eel?

A snake is a reptile; an eel is a fish. They look so similar because this type of long, thin body is very useful for many different ways of life.

What kind of animal was a dinosaur?

A reptile. Living reptiles include lizards, snakes, turtles, tortoises and crocodiles. None of these is closely related to the dinosaurs.

What was the largest animal that ever lived?

It was probably a dinosaur called *Seismosaurus* ('earth-shaking lizard') whose fossilized bones were discovered in New Mexico, USA. *Seismosaurus* may have been as much as 40 metres long. It was only discovered recently, and before that the Blue Whale was thought to be the largest animal of all time. It is possible that this living animal *does* outdo *Seismosaurus* in sheer weight, because much of the dinosaur's length was taken up by its long neck and tail.

What was the largest bird that ever lived?

The Elephant Bird, or Roc, of Madagascar. It stood more than three metres tall and was massively built, probably weighing over 400 kilograms. Not surprisingly, this feathered heavyweight was unable to fly. The Roc is not, strictly speaking, prehistoric, because it probably survived until the 17th century. The same is true of the New Zealand Moas, one of which was actually taller than the Roc, at four metres.

What is the shell of a Sea Urchin called?

The shell of a Sea Urchin is formed inside its body, and for this reason it is called a test. When a Sea Urchin dies, all its spines drop off, leaving the familiar decorative test which is often sold in gift shops.

What was the name of the first dinosaur to be discovered?

Megalosaurus, which literally means 'great lizard'. William Buckland described this huge flesh-eating dinosaur in 1824, which had a large head, saw-edged teeth and powerful back legs.

What was an ichthyosaur?

An ichthyosaur was a fish-like reptile – its name means 'fish-lizard'. It lived over 280 million years ago, and looked something like a sharp-nosed dolphin, although the two animals are not related.

Which dinosaur looked like a three-horned rhinoceros?

Triceratops – although Triceratops was much bigger than our more familiar rhinoceros. Triceratops grew up to nine metres long, and had a bony frill around its neck. It lived in herds, and used its horns in self-defence.

What do Crab-eating Foxes eat?

Crabs are just one item on the daily menu of this shy, nocturnal animal. It also likes rodents, insects, fruits, berries, lizards and eggs.

If you wanted to be preserved as a fossil, what would you do?

You would have to choose a spot to die in very carefully. The best place would be an estuary, where a river flows into the sea. The estuary brings down sediment which would cover up your body quickly. After millions of years the sediment would have turned into rock, with your bones safely inside it. The bottom of the sea or a river, or a cave would also be good, because sediments build up in these places too.

WHERE?

Where do Marsh Tits live?

Marsh Tits don't live in marshland as you might expect, they prefer dense broadleaved woodland, usually with oak, hornbeam and beech trees. The misnomer arose from the time when it was confused with the Willow Tit, a very similar-looking bird, with a preference for marshy, damp woodland.

Where will you find lemurs?

Lemurs can only be found in the wild on the island of Madagascar, off the east coast of Africa. There are about 16 different species of lemur, and most live in dense woodland.

Where do herons make their nests?

Despite spending most of their time wading in shallow water looking for fish, herons make their large conspicuous nests in trees, alongside the nests of other herons.

Where do Black Grouse perform their courtship ritual?

Male and female Black Grouse do not form pairs but meet only for the purpose of mating. Males will display on the same patch of moorland which has been used year after year by generations of birds. Often the dominant male (the one who holds the prime position on the display ground or *lek*) will mate with 80 per cent of the females.

Where do swallows fly each autumn?

Swallows breed in Europe in the summer, but to escape the harsh winter they fly south, as far as southern Africa.

Where do Elf Owls roost during the day?

Elf Owls are among the smallest of owls. These Mexican birds will often roost and built their nests in cactus plants, using the abandoned holes of Gila Woodpeckers.

Where will you find a wild yak?

Yaks are large sturdy animals with long, thick woolly coats to enable them to withstand extreme cold. They live on the high plateaux of Tibet and Kashmir, where they eke out an existence on the mountain tundra.

Where do situngas hide during the day?

Situngas are large, solitary antelopes from central and western Africa. They feed on marshland plants by night, and during the day will hide in reed swamps. If danger threatens, they will sink into the swamp mud, so that only their nostrils show

Where do Fallow Deer hide their young?

Female Fallow Deer or does hide their fawns in the long grass or bracken of the woodland floor. The mother will move away or back to the herd to feed, but return at regular intervals to suckle her fawn.

Where are you most likely to find a scorpion?

Scorpions are common inhabitants of hot deserts. They shelter from the heat in crevices or under rocks during the day, and come out at night to hunt.

Where does Przewalzki's Horse roam?

This wild horse, the ancestor of the domestic horse, is so rare now that it may soon become extinct. Herds of these horses used to roam the plains of Mongolia and western China, each herd being led by a single dominant male.

Where were Ghost Frogs first discovered?

Ghost Frogs do not look at all ghostly – they were given their name when a species was discovered in Skeleton Gorge in South Africa.

Where will you find Golden Eagles?

Golden Eagles are birds of mountain and moorland, and are widely distributed throughout the northern hemisphere. Persecution by humans and the effect of pesticides on their egg shells (making them extremely fragile) have caused large depletions in their numbers.

Where do cowbirds lay their eggs?

Cowbirds have a reputation for being even lazier than cuckoos – not only do they lay their eggs in the nests of other birds, but they also rely on cattle to help supplement their diet. The insects disturbed by the cattle's feet or attracted to the animal's hide provide the birds with an easy meal.

Where would you look for an Apollo Butterfly?

Apollos are beautiful, large, white butterflies with a slow, fluttering flight. They used to be widespread in mountainous regions of Europe and Asia, but populations are now small and isolated.

Where do the eggs of the South American Marsupial Frog develop?

The eggs of this tree-dwelling frog develop in a special skin pouch on the female's back. As the female lays her eggs, she bends forward so that they roll down her back. The male fertilizes them before they become embedded in her pouch.

Where do Saiga Antelope go in winter?

Saiga Antelope graze the treeless plains (steppes) of Asia, well protected from the wind by their thick heavy coats. In the autumn large herds gather for the annual migration southwards in search of food and more clement weather.

Where do nightjars sleep during the day?

Nightjars sleep on the ground during the day, either on the woodland floor or on moorland, among the bracken and heather. They are so well camouflaged, and sleep so perfectly still, that they are very difficult to spot.

Where does a hamster store its food?

Hamsters are small rodents with large cheek pouches, which they fill with nuts and seeds as they go about looking for food. It is not until they return to their nest that they unpack their pouches, and sort out the night's finds.

Where does eiderdown come from?

Eider Ducks give us eiderdown – the soft warm filling we associate with quilts and feather pillows. The Eider Duck is a bird of the Arctic north: when the female makes her nest she lines it with the soft feathers plucked from her breast.

Where does the anaconda catch its prey?

The anaconda is more of a passive hunter than an active one. This river-dwelling snake, one of the largest living snakes, lies in wait in murky waters, ready to attack animals and birds that come to the water to drink.

Where do North American Desert Ants store 'honey'?

The North American Desert Ants have contrived a most ingenious method of storing the sugary liquid that they collect from oak apples. They feed a number of worker ants with the juice until their abdomens swell up like balloons. These worker ants provide living storage containers for the rest of the colony, and are tapped in the months to come for the sweet contents of their abdomens.

Where did the dodo used to live?

The dodo used to live on the islands of Mauritius and Reunion to the east of Madagascar in the Indian Ocean. This curious flightless bird became extinct in the 18th century due to overhunting by humans and the introduction of cats, dogs and pigs to the islands (for which the dodo and its eggs made easy prey).

Where do domestic dogs come from?

The ancestors of domestic dogs were probably wolves or jackals, who first formed a partnership with humans over 10,000 years ago. Dogs were the first animals to be domesticated by human beings.

Where are the Galapagos Islands?

The Galapagos Islands are a small group of islands of volcanic origin found in the Pacific Ocean, 900 kilometres west of Ecuador. They became famous after a visit by Charles Darwin in 1835.

Where do Gall Wasps lay their eggs?

Gall Wasps lay their eggs in the buds of oak trees, giving rise to the 'oak apples' so commonly seen on oak trees. The 'apple' develops to protect the white grub inside.

Where would you look for the biggest butterfly in the world?

The Queen Alexandra Birdwing Butterfly is the largest and heaviest butterfly in the world. It is unfortunately extremely rare, and is restricted to a small area of rainforest in Papua New Guinea.

Where do Fairy Terns lay their eggs?

It is something of a puzzle as to why Fairy Terns do not make nests, because there is plenty of nesting material on the tropical islands where they live. The Fairy Tern lays her single egg either on bare ground or on a forked branch high in a tree. The young chick is born with very sharp claws which help it to cling on to its perch until it can fly.

Where do Pink Fairy Armadillos live?

Pink Fairy Armadillos spend most of their lives underground in a burrow, venturing out at night to hunt for insects. At the first indication of danger, they quickly retreat into their burrows.

Where do Sand Gobies build their nests?

Sand Gobies are small fish which build their nests on the sea floor using the abandoned shell of a bivalve (hinged mollusc).

Where did life begin?

Life probably began in the sea. That is why all living things contain water. Our blood still has a similar composition to seawater in terms of mineral salts.

Where do Guinea Pigs come from?

Guinea Pigs come from South America, where their wild ancestors, the brown cavies, live in small groups in rocky grasslands. They are stocky, nocturnal animals, the size of large rats, and sleep in burrows during the day.

Where did the herbivorous dinosaurs find enough grass to eat?

Not all dinosaurs were meat-eaters, some did feed on plants. But they did not eat grass, because there was no grass to eat! The grasses are relatively new plants which did not evolve until after the dinosaurs died out.

Where were the fossilized remains of Archaeopteryx first discovered?

Archaeopteryx is the name given to a creature that was half bird, half reptile, and lived about 150 million years ago. Its remains were first discovered in limestone caves in Solnhofen, Bavaria in 1861.

Where do we find living animals that are direct descendents of dinosaurs?

The birds. They evolved from a species of small dinosaur that took to the trees and then gradually developed the ability to fly. The fossil *Archaeopteryx* shows what the early ancestors of birds looked like. They had wings and feathers like a bird, but they still had teeth, and a long lizard-like tail.

Where is the group of islands that inspired Darwin's theory of evolution?

The Galapagos Islands, off the west coast of South America. Darwin found that only certain types of animals had managed to reach these islands from the mainland. This made the islands a 'laboratory for evolution' where all sorts of unusual creatures could evolve without interference. Birds like the Galapagos Finches were obviously all descended from a single parent species but they had evolved into many different species.

What are the largest animals on the Galapagos Islands?

Giant Tortoises whose shells can measure up to 1.2 metres in length. Darwin found that they had a different type of shell pattern on each island. The tortoises were all descended from common ancestors, which had probably floated there from the South American mainland on logs. But the tortoises had later become isolated from each other on the different islands.

WHEN?

When did Charles Darwin set out on his famous voyage around the world?

Charles Darwin secured a position as naturalist on HMS *Beagle* and set off on his voyage of discovery on 27 December 1831.

When do Grunion Fish lay their eggs?

The Californian Grunion Fish waits for a full or new moon before laying its eggs. On the high tide shoals of grunion come ashore to lay, fertilize and bury their eggs in the sand, before being swept back out to sea again by the waves. The eggs lie dormant in the sand until the next spring tide uncovers them, which stimulates hatching and the young fish larvae swim away.

When did the first mammals appear?

The first mammals were tiny shrew-like creatures that appeared 200 million years ago at the same time as the dinosaurs were evolving. When the dinosaurs became extinct, the mammals took over.

When is the best time to watch badgers?

The best time to watch badgers is at sunrise or dusk, for they spend most of the day out of sight, hidden within their burrow or set. You should position yourself downwind of their set and keep as quiet and as still as you can.

When do peacocks shed their tail feathers?

Peacocks shed their brilliant tail feathers at the end of the breeding season.

When did the first human beings walk the land?

Our ancestors, the early humans, first started to live on the ground (in preference to the trees) about 14 million years ago. Walking upright followed soon after.

When do sloths come down from the trees?

Sloths spend most of their inactive lives hanging upside down in the trees, feasting on *Crecorpia* leaves. They do come down from their lofty hiding places about once a week to urinate and defecate – and they always use the same place to do this.

When was the last Ice Age?

The last Ice Age occurred about 19,000 years ago, when ice covered much of Europe, Asia and North America.

When did the Passenger Pigeon become extinct?

Millions of Passenger Pigeons once inhabited the eastern forests of North America, but sadly, due to overhunting and habitat loss, their numbers declined drastically during the 19th century. The last captive Passenger Pigeon died in Cincinnati Zoo in 1914.

When did Noah build his ark?

Noah is an Old Testament figure who is supposed to have built an ark not long after God created the world. Apparently God became sorry that he had created people because they were so wicked, and so resolved to destroy them all with a great flood. However, he wanted to spare Noah as he was a good man, and so ordered him to build an ark and to fill it with two animals – a male and female – of every kind.

When was the Great Plague of London?

The Great Plague claimed over 70,000 lives when it swept through the city during the summer of 1665. This infectious disease was passed on to humans by rat fleas.

When was myxomatosis introduced into Britain?

Myxomatosis is an infectious disease of rabbits which was introduced into Britain during the 1950s in an attempt to control the rabbit population.

When did the dinosaurs become extinct?

65 million years ago. No-one is sure whether they all died out very quickly, or whether it took thousands of years. Much of the evidence supports the idea of a giant meteorite hitting the Earth at about this time. This would have thrown up a huge amount of dust into the atmosphere, blocking the Sun's rays and caused a disastrous change in climate. Other very successful animals became extinct at the same time as the dinosaurs and the fact that they all died out together suggests that a change in climate is the most likely explanation.

When was the Age of the Reptiles?

Reptiles dominated the land for about 215 million years, from 280 to 65 million years ago. The reptiles which are alive today represent only a small fraction of the total number of reptiles which once existed.

When did the first fish appear in the oceans?

Fish were the first true vertebrates – that is, they were the first animals to have a backbone. They appeared about 430 million years ago.

When did Neanderthal Man live?

Between about 125,000 and 25,000 years ago, during the ice ages.

When do limpets go for a walk?

After dark. They lift their shells then and move about the rocks in search of food. Because the Sun is down they are in less danger of drying out, and at less risk from predators such as gulls.

When does the Palolo Worm of Samoa breed?

During the last quarter of the moon in October. The worms, which live in burrows in coral, release parts of their bodies containing eggs and sperm then. Like many other animals in the sea, they use the moon to help them time their breeding season.

When did the last Giant Sloths die out?

The Giant Ground Sloth or *Megatherium* became extinct about 10–11,000 years ago.

When did Cane Toads arrive in Australia?

In 1935, when sugar-cane growers were plagued by Cane Beetles, and hoped that the toads, natives of Central and South America, would eat these pests. With no enemies to keep their numbers down, the toads are now a pest in Queensland.

When did life begin?

No one really knows when life on Earth began, but it was probably between 3500 million and 4000 million years ago.

When was *Archaeopteryx* discovered?

The first fossil that was recognized as *Archaeopteryx* was found in 1861 by workmen in a limestone quarry in Germany. Other fossils had been found before then, but had been classified as ordinary dinosaurs, because the impression of the feathers was not present (only in very fine rocks are the feathers preserved). A number of other *Archaeopteryx* fossils have been found since 1861.

When do swallows fly south?

In late summer, for those that breed in the northern hemisphere and winter in the tropics. For those that breed in the southern hemisphere, such as the Welcome Swallow of Australia, the southward flight comes in the early spring.

When did reptiles take to the air?

On two occasions, once about 220 million years ago, when the pterosaurs (or pterodactyls) evolved, and again about 150 million years ago, when the ancestors of birds appeared.

When did the amphibians evolve?

About 370 million years ago, when fish which already had lungs for breathing air, and fleshy fins, began to move out onto the land, probably in search of food.

When did Iguanodon live?

Between about 130 and 110 million years ago. During this time Iguanodon was very common, and probably lived in large herds.

WHY?

Why do lizards sit on white walls?

Lizards are cold-blooded animals which take their warmth from the sun and their surroundings. The colour white reflects the sunlight well, and the lizard soaks up this reflected heat.

Why do frogs have pale bellies?

When frogs swim through the water, their pale undersides help to camouflage them against the light filtering through the water. If the frogs had dark bellies, they would be easy to see by their underwater enemies.

Why do Fat-tailed Dunnarts have fat tails?

The Fat-tailed Dunnart is a mouse-like marsupial from Australia. Its tail is fat because during the rainy season it stores surplus fat there, to carry it through periods of drought.

Why do desmans have flattened tails?

Desmans may be thought of as water-dwelling moles, with long whiffly noses, webbed feet and large, flattened tails. They use their tails both as a rudder and a means of propulsion.

Why do toucans have such large beaks?

Nobody knows the real reason why toucans have such prominent beaks: it could be that they serve as important visual signals during courtship, or they may help the bird to grasp food that would otherwise be out of reach. Despite their large size, their beaks are amazingly light, being constructed of a honeycomb of bony tissue.

Why are Burnet Moths so colourful?

Burnet Moths are brightly coloured (usually red on black) to advertise to birds how horrible they taste. So repugnant are they that once a bird has eaten one, it is careful not to make the same mistake again.

Why do animals have territories?

The marking out of territories by animals provides a very useful service to the population of a species as a whole. Firstly, it ensures that the animals don't suffer from overcrowding, and secondly, that there is enough food to go round.

Why do some lizards lick their eggs?

Some lizards use their sense of taste and smell to identify their own brood. The licking enables the mother, after she has been away from the nest, to recognize her own eggs.

Why do we say 'as mad as a March Hare'?

This expression has arisen because of the extraordinary behaviour of male Brown Hares during March and April. At this time (prior to the breeding season), they race around the countryside, fighting with other males in dramatic boxing displays. They rise up on their hindlegs and batter each other with their forepaws. The male hare is also said to have mad staring eyes, although this is simply a quality of their large, rather glassy eyes.

Why do certain orchids look like insects?

It is no accident that certain orchids, such as the Fly and Bee Orchids, resemble the bodies of insects, for it is a means by which they achieve pollination. Male insects are deceived into thinking that these orchids are the females of their species, and attempt to 'mate' with the flowers, collecting pollen in the process. This pollen is transferred when the insect tries to mate with another orchid.

Why do hyenas laugh?

Hyenas are sociable, co-operative animals which also happen to be very noisy. The eerie laugh for which they are well known is often heard just as they go in for the kill – an excited but jubilant cacophany of sound.

Why do giraffes have such long necks?

Giraffes have long necks to enable them to feed from branches that are inaccessible to other herbivores. Their long necks also allow them to see danger long before it reaches them.

Why does the Blue-crowned Hanging Parrot sleep upside down?

The Blue-crowned Hanging Parrot sleeps upside down in order to make itself as inconspicuous as possible. Its predominantly green plumage blends in well with the green foliage, so that it looks just like another leaf.

Why is the Black Mamba snake so feared?

The African Black Mamba is a large, slender, highly venomous snake capable of moving at speeds of up to 23 kilometres per hour. It can move as fast as a human and its bite may be fatal.

Why do tortoises urinate on the sand covering their eggs?

The strong-smelling urine of the tortoise either prevents predators from sniffing out their eggs, or makes them unpalatable to any animal who might otherwise be tempted to dig them up.

Why do African Black Herons hold their wings out while feeding?

By spreading its wings out to form a canopy, the Black Heron creates an area of shade over the water immediately in front of it. The shaded area may attract fish who believe they are swimming into cover, or it may help the heron to spot fish more easily.

Why do female and not male mosquitoes suck blood from warm-blooded animals?

Without a drink of blood from a warm-blooded vertebrate, the eggs of the female mosquito are unable to mature. The male mosquito is content to suck plant juices.

Why do squids squirt ink?

Squids squirt ink to escape the attentions of any would-be predator. If a large fish approaches a squid, it will squirt out a blob of black ink and retreat immediately, changing colour as it does so. The ink does not disperse right away, but retains its shape for a few seconds – long enough to confuse the fish and give the squid time to make its escape.

Why do Eyed Hawkmoths have 'eyes' on their wings?

An Eyed Hawkmoth will fall to the ground and display two large eye-spots on its hindwings if it senses danger. This behaviour will scare away many of its potential enemies.

Why do Spitting Cobras spit?

Spitting Cobras spit either to defend themselves or to attack a potential foe. The 'spit' is actually venom forcibly shot out from its fangs in two jets, which the snake aims at its opponent's eyes in an attempt to blind it.

Why does the Upside-down Catfish swim upside down?

This African freshwater fish swims upside down in order to feed off the algae which grow on the underside of fallen leaves.

Why do Slipper Limpets pile up on top of each other?

Slipper Limpets commonly live in stacks of several individuals, each one fastened on to the lower one's back. This peculiar piling behaviour results from the limpet's ability to change sex during its lifetime. The first limpet to settle becomes a female, attracting a male to settle on her back. However, the male limpet will change into a female as he grows older, causing another male to settle on his/her back. Thus the pile of limpets consists of females towards the bottom, males at the top, and limpets of both sexes in the middle!

Why do African Elephants have large ears?

An African Elephant uses its large ears as a means of keeping cool. They act like radiators to give off excess body heat.

Why do Herring Gulls have a red spot on their beaks?

The red spot on the lower part of the Herring Gull's beak acts as a stimulus to its chicks. Persistent pecking at this spot by the chicks prompts the parent into regurgitating food for them.

Why do we yawn?

We yawn when we are tired, and the very act of doing so causes our lungs to fill with air. This in turn increases the supply of oxygen to our blood, and the greater flow of oxygenated blood to our muscles has the effect of reducing tiredness.

Why do pilotfish follow sharks?

Pilotfish accompany sharks mainly because they find it easier to swim in the slipstream of a larger fish. They also gain a certain immunity from attack by predators who would rather keep well out of the way of the shark's fearsome jaws. At feeding times, too, the pilotfish benefits from any scraps not eaten by the shark.

Why do geese fly in formation?

Geese fly in formation not to look neat, but as a means of conserving energy by flying in the slipstream of the bird in front of them. Occasionally the leading bird, who gains no advantage from this, will drop back and allow another bird to take its place.

Why do Hermit Crabs encourage Sea Anemones to grow on their shells?

Hermit Crabs gain a certain amount of protection from the stinging cells of the Sea Anemone, while the Sea Anemone sweeps up any scraps left over from the crab when it feeds. The Sea Anemone also helps to camouflage the crab on the sea bed.

Why do Saiga Antelope have big noses?

The Saiga Antelope of the Russian steppes have enlarged, downward-pointing noses to help them cope with the cold and dusty environment in which they live. Their noses are copiously lined with hairs and mucous glands, which serve to filter out the dust stirred up by large herds as they tramp across the thin soils, and also warm up the cold air as it is inhaled.

Why are old male gorillas called silverbacks?

Old male gorillas tend to have silvery-grey hair on their backs – hence the name.

Why do some birds build their nests right next to a wasps' nest?

Certain tropical weaverbirds choose to have wasps as their neighbours because of the protection they receive should any predator attempt to rob their nests. For some reason the wasps do not mind the birds living so near.

Why do some sharks allow small fish to enter their mouths?

Certain sharks will allow cleaner fish to enter their mouths in order to be rid of their irksome mouth parasites. When the cleaner fish has completed its task the shark will allow it to depart unmolested.

Why do spoonbills have long beaks which are flattened at the tip?

Spoonbills find the shape of their beaks just right for sweeping up small fish, crustaceans and worms that live in shallow water. These birds probably rely on their beaks rather than their eyesight to detect prey, as the ends of their beaks are very sensitive to any movement in the water.

Why are storks thought to be lucky birds?

According to legend, storks are the bringers of babies, and so the stork has always been regarded with some affection.

Why do birds shift and turn their eggs in the nest?

Nesting birds, particularly those with large clutches, may be seen at regular intervals shifting and poking their eggs about with their beaks. They do this to ensure that the temperature of all the eggs is kept even.

Why did people dance frantically if they'd been bitten by a tarantula?

A tarantula is a large hairy spider with a poisonous bite which used to be thought fatal. According to folklore, the only cure for the bite of the tarantula was to dance until you dropped, to sweat the poison out of your body. The name of this dance was the tarantella.

Why do birds remove empty eggshells from the nest?

Parent birds remove empty eggshells because they are white and conspicuous to predators. Some birds may be observed carrying their empty shells some distance from the nest before dropping them.

Why do Atlas Moths have large, feathery antennae?

Only the males have large feathery antennae, and they use them to detect the scent of a female. So sensitive are their antennae, that only one scent molecule per cubic metre of air may be necessary to stimulate the males into searching for the females.

Why do swordfish have such elongated snouts?

Nobody knows for sure why the swordfish has developed such a pronounced 'sword'. It could be that the fish uses it to strike at other fish, or it may simply have evolved as a response to body stream-lining.

Why is the Honey Possum's tongue long and bristly at the tip?

The Australian Honey Possum uses its tongue to probe into the flowers of *Banksia*, to extract the pollen and nectar.

Why does the Giant Anteater have a bushy tail?

The Giant Anteater's distinctive bushy tail is a useful implement for sweeping up the termites it scatters when it breaks open one of their nests. It may also use its tail as a sunshade when sleeping out in the open.

Why are Howler Monkeys so noisy?

The South American Howler Monkeys have specially enlarged larynxes which enable them to shout long and loud at other Howler Monkeys – in fact, they are so loud that they may be heard at distances of over three kilometres. The purpose of all this shouting is to establish territorial boundaries.

Why do tarsiers have such large eyes?

Tarsiers are small, nocturnal, meat-eating creatures from the forests of south-east Asia. Their large eyes have pupils capable of opening so wide that they dominate the centre of the eye. Such large pupils enable Tarsiers to see their prey in the dimmest of light.

Why are cormorants on the Galapagos Islands unable to fly?

Cormorants from the Galapagos Islands lost the ability to fly simply because they did not need to. Before humans arrived on the scene the Galapagos cormorants had no natural predators.

Why do Spadefoot Toads breed in a hurry?

Spadefoot Toads breed only during the rainy season in temporary rainpools. This means that all the business of reproduction, and the formation of the tadpole has to be carried out before the rainpools dry up. Some species of Spadefoot Toad can do all this within two weeks.

Why do Baya Weaver Birds have long entrance funnels to their nests?

The nest of the Asian Baya Weaver Bird is spherical with a long entrance funnel at the bottom. This funnel is to stop predatory snakes from getting inside.

Why are the undersides of a butterfly's wings dull and mottled?

Butterflies are easy to see as they fly about because of their brightly coloured wings. When they land butterflies hold their wing vertically, hiding the distinctive patterns, and showing only the dull brownish undersides. This camouflages the insect, making it safer from hungry predators.

Why do Bighorn Sheep have such large spiral horns?

The massive curved horns of the Bighorn Sheep are mainly used as a measure of a male's rank and dominance within the herd. The larger the horns, the more dominant the male.

Why do Sperm Whales have such huge heads?

The head of a Sperm Whale is huge in proportion to the rest of its body, accounting for at least a third of its total length. Much of its head is given over to special wax-filled organs (known as *spermaceti* organs) which help regulate the whale's buoyancy when it dives.

Why are the chicks of the Hoatzin Bird so good at climbing trees?

The South American Hoatzin Bird is an odd-looking bird, with a scraggy neck and small crested head. Its chicks are born with a unique feature which is lost in the adult. They have a pair of hooked claws on the bend of each wing, which makes them good at clambering about in trees.

Why is the lower half of the skimmer's beak longer than the upper half?

The lower half of the skimmer's beak is almost a third as long again as the upper half. This unique adaptation allows the skimmer to pluck fish from the water by flying close to the surface and lowering its bottom beak into the water. It snaps shut when it touches a fish.

Why do cranes dance?

Cranes are extremely rare birds with long beaks, long necks, and long legs. These elegant birds are perhaps best known for their elaborate dancing rituals, which help to cement the bond between a breeding couple. Sometimes a flock of cranes will dance for no apparent reason other than sheer pleasure.

Why were oarfish at one time thought to be 'sea serpents'?

An oarfish is a very unusual-looking fish. Its body is flat like a long silvery ribbon with a red dorsal fin that runs the entire length of its body. It swims by rippling its body through the water, and it is capable of growing up to seven metres long. With such odd features it is not surprising that it gave rise to the sea serpent legends of long ago.

Why do Great Crested Grebes eat their own feathers?

Nobody knows the real reason why Great Crested Grebes pluck and eat their own feathers, although it has been suggested that the feathers help in the formation of pellets. The pellets consist of everything, such as fish bones, that the grebe cannot digest.

Why are Mountain Goats so surefooted?

Mountain Goats rarely fall from their precarious mountain ledges because their hard hooves have a central spongy pad which gives them amazingly good grip on slippery rocks and ice.

Why is the Openbill Bird unable to shut its beak properly?

The Openbill of southern Asia is a member of the stork family, and its beak is most unusual in that it only meets at the tips. This peculiar feature seems to suit the bird well for catching and holding freshwater snails.

Why are rhinoceros horns so highly prized?

Rhinoceros horns fetch large sums of money on the black market, for they are used to make handles for ceremonial daggers in countries such as North Yemen.

Why is the woodpecker called the carpenter of the forest?

Of all the birds, only the woodpecker is properly equipped for the business of woodworking. Using its strong, straight beak it is able to chisel out a nesting hole in a tree trunk, gripping on to the bark with its strong claws and bracing itself from behind with its stiff tail feathers.

Why do pronghorns have white rumps?

The pronghorn is a fast-running, deer-like creature of the American prairie. The white hairs on its rump stand up if the animal senses danger, flashing an alarm signal to other pronghorns.

Why do roadrunners run rather than fly?

Roadrunners can fly as well as run, but they are much better at running, and prefer to use this method of getting about. Roadrunners may sometimes be observed dashing across roads in arid parts of North America, attaining speeds of up to 24 kilometres per hour.

Why do Frogmouth Birds have bristly feathers around their beaks?

When perched motionless on a tree stump with its beak pointing upwards, the Frogmouth is very difficult to distinguish from the stump on which it is sitting. The bristly feathers help to blur the sharp outline of its beak.

Why do cormorants perch on rocks with their wings outspread?

The cormorant is a diving bird, and to help it sink quickly its feathers are specially constructed to allow water to penetrate them easily. After diving, it holds its wings out to dry.

Why do oysters make pearls?

Oysters make pearls in response to an invasion of their body by a small piece of foreign matter. The oyster secretes thin layers of mother-of-pearl around the foreign body, which build up over the years into a pearl.

Why is the quetzal regarded as a sacred bird?

The ancient Mayan and Aztec civilizations of Mexico viewed the brilliantly coloured quetzal as a sacred bird because of its links with the plumed serpent god. Its long tail feathers were sought after for use in ceremonies.

Why is the Vine Snake so thin?

Not only is the Vine Snake of South America long and thin, it is also greenish brown, making it virtually indistinguishable from the vines and creepers in which it lives.

Why do monkeys groom each other?

Monkeys groom each other to rid themselves of dirt and dry skin. They also do it as a way of making and maintaining friendships.

Why does the Hooded Seal have such a big nose?

The Hooded Seal of the Arctic Ocean has a large fleshy sac on the end of its nose which can be blown up like a balloon. The Male Hooded seal will inflate his nasal sac during the breeding season, both to attract females and intimidate rival males.

Why do cats' eyes shine in the dark?

Cats have a shiny layer called a *tapetum* at the back of their eyes, and it is this layer which glows when light shines on them in the dark.

Why do ostriches have wings?

It is well known that ostriches cannot fly, and yet their wings are large and adorned with soft, curling feathers. The ostrich uses its wings both to balance with when running at high speed, and in courtship displays.

Why do some lovebirds have brush-like feathers on their rumps?

African Lovebirds are renowned for their affectionate mutual preening behaviour, which they perform with their beaks. Their brush-like tail feathers are used for carrying nesting material back to the nest site, leaving the birds' beaks free for preening.

Why do camels have long eyelashes?

A camel's long eyelashes help to protect its eyes during desert sandstorms.

Why do Green Turtles lay so many eggs?

Green Turtles may lay several clutches of over a hundred eggs each during the breeding season, but there is a high death rate among young turtles. When the young turtles hatch out and dig their way out of their sandy nests on the beach, they face a hazardous journey to the sea, past many hungry predators.

Why do the leaves of rose bushes sometimes have pale wiggly lines on them?

These pale meandering lines are the trails made by the caterpillars of certain leaf-mining insects, who are so small that they can eat between the upper and lower surfaces of the leaf. As the caterpillars grow the trail becomes wider.

Why do hippopotamuses like water?

Water not only helps to keep a hippopotamus clean and cool in hot climates, but it also supports its great weight, making it easier to move around.

Why are chameleons said to have the best all-round vision of any reptile?

Chameleons have the extraordinary ability to move and focus their eyes independently of each other. Bulging out on either side of the head, the eyes swivel round in search of prey, and on sighting a suitable victim, both eyes then work together to give the chameleon a clearer view.

What makes the female Ghost Moth so different from other female insects?

The Ghost Moth is one of the few insects known where the female flies in pursuit of the male. It is far more normal for the females to remain static or sluggish in courtship and for the males to seek them out. The male Ghost Moth has shining white wings and performs a hovering courtship dance to attract the duller yellow females.

Why is the world's smallest antelope called the Royal Antelope?

The Royal Antelope of west Africa is not much bigger than a rabbit, and weighs about the same – four kilograms. Local tribespeople know this deer as the 'king of the hares', which is why European scientists called it the 'royal' antelope.

Why do crocodiles swallow stones?

Crocodiles swallow stones to help them sink to the bottom of a river more easily.

Why is the Grey Squirrel considered to be a pest?

The Grey Squirrel is looked on as a pest because it destroys the bark of beech, oak and sycamore trees, and will also feed on cereal crops.

Why is the mink sometimes mistaken for an otter?

Observers of the river bank quite commonly mistake a mink for an otter, although if you were to see them close up, there would be little confusion. Otters are significantly larger, with broader, flatter heads, and tend to be shy, solitary creatures. Unfortunately otters are now very rare.

Why do Desert Tortoises have large bladders?

Desert Tortoises sometimes spray their rear ends with urine as a mean of keeping cool if they are in danger of becoming overheated. Frightened tortoises may also spray urine in self-defence.

Why are Red Deer careful not to knock their antlers while they are in velvet?

Because they are extremely sensitive at this stage. The 'velvet' is actually skin which is richly supplied with blood vessels and covered in fine hairs. It is responsible for forming the bone of the antlers. Only when the antlers are fully formed do they lose their sensitivity (and the 'velvet).

Why do turtles return to land to lay their eggs?

Turtles, like all reptiles, lay eggs, but because they are not waterproof the eggs must be laid on dry land so that the developing embryo can breathe. Every breeding season the female turtle has to return to coastal waters and haul herself up on to the beach, where she digs a hole to lay her eggs.

Why were Woolly Rhinoceroses woolly?

Woolly Rhinoceroses lived during the Ice Ages and needed a fur coat to keep warm. The same applied to shaggy, long-haired elephants, known as Woolly Mammoths.

HOW?

How many animals are in danger of extinction?

The number is frighteningly large. If humans persist in destroying tropical forests and poisoning the environment, we could lose well over a million species by the end of this century. Many of these species will become extinct without us ever having known them.

How much tropical forest is being destroyed each year?

Each year some 12 million hectares of tropical forest – an area almost the size of England – are cut down or set alight, either to supply wood to the commercial logger, or to make way for cattle ranchers.

How does the Frilled Lizard react to danger?

The Frilled Lizard of Australia responds to danger by opening its mouth wide and hissing, and erecting its large frill-like collar. In this way it hopes to frighten off any attackers.

How did the Secretary Bird get its name?

The African Secretary Bird gets its name from the long, black-tipped plume-like feathers at the back of its head, which are said to resemble the quill pens used by secretaries many years ago.

How poisonous is the Black Widow Spider?

The bite of the Black Widow Spider is extremely painful and can be lethal if not treated promptly. Fortunately these spiders are shy creatures and will only bite under provocation. The males rarely, if ever, bite.

How does an okapi clean its eyes?

The tongue of an okapi is so long that it uses it to clean its own eyes and eyelids.

How many tentacles does a star-nosed mole have on its nose?

No fewer than 22 tentacles sit on the end of the Star-nosed Mole's nose. They help the mole to find its prey.

How do giraffes feed from the ground?

Giraffes have such long legs that, despite the length of their necks, they are unable to feed or drink easily from the ground. They get round this by splaying their legs so that their shoulders are lowered, and their heads can reach the ground.

How do kingsnakes kill rattlesnakes?

Kingsnakes are immune to rattlesnake venom, and will kill rattlesnakes by coiling their bodies around them and suffocating them.

How do Click Beetles escape from danger?

Click Beetles have a habit of suddenly jerking themselves up into the air to escape the attentions of a predator. As the beetle lurches upwards it makes a clicking sound which is the sound of the spring mechanism between the thorax and abdomen being released.

How did bushbabies get their name?

Not only do bushbabies look very endearing, with their enormous eyes and furry bodies, but they also sound endearing too, with a cry that sounds remarkably like a human baby.

How do woodpeckers break open nuts?

Woodpeckers are very skilful at breaking open nuts, by using a 'woodpecker's anvil'. This may be a crevice or crack in the tree bark into which the nut is wedged, allowing the woodpecker to tackle the nut with its strong beak.

How does the addax survive in the desert without drinking?

The addax antelope is amazingly economical in its use of water. It obtains all the liquid it needs from the plants it eats.

How do Paradise Tree Snakes climb up trees?

Paradise Tree Snakes have a series of ridged scales on their bellies which help them to grip on to any roughened surface. This helps them to climb trees with astonishing ease.

How do Water Spiders breathe under water?

The Water Spider breathes under water by constructing its own pocket of air. This pocket or bell is made of silk, and the spider laboriously fills it with air by repeatedly carrying bubbles of air below the surface of the water.

How big is a Goliath Beetle?

Compared with other insects, Goliath Beetles are enormous. Male beetles can grow up to 15 centimetres long, and weigh around 70–100 grams. They would easily fill the palm of your hand.

How do birds know when to start nesting?

Birds are prompted to build nests by the gradual lengthening of the days. Daylight stimulates them to release substances called hormones into the bloodstream. These hormones in turn stimulate the birds to behave in certain ways – one of which is to start nestbuilding.

How does the sandgrouse provide its chicks with water?

The sandgrouse is a bird of semi-desert, and because of the lack of moisture in its diet, it needs to drink every day. It takes water to its chicks by soaking its belly feathers in water, and then allowing them to drink from its feathers as it stands upright in the nest.

How strong are the webs of the Nephila Spider?

The webs of the Nephila Spider are so strong that people have been known to make fishing nets out of them. It is not unusual for the Nephila Spider to catch small birds in its web, which it then kills and eats.

How does the Snail-eating Snake extract snails from their shells?

The Snail-eating Snake has a long lower jaw lined with curved teeth, which it sinks into the snail's soft body. It then pulls its lower jaw backwards, winkling the snail out of its shell as it does so.

How do mongooses kill snakes?

Mongooses have a natural immunity to cobra poison, but not to other snake venoms. Therefore when attacking snakes they rely mainly on speed, agility and their dense fur for protection. They seize the snake behind the head and shake it to death.

How do oilbirds find their way in the dark?

Oilbirds live in dark caves in South America and, rather like bats, they rely on a system of echo-location to find their way about. As they fly they give out a series of high-pitched clicks, and listen for the echoes to determine what's around them.

How does the Alpine Water Skink keep active in cold weather?

This small Australian lizard can keep active even when its body temperature drops to below freezing. This is because it has a small quantity of glycerol in its blood, which acts as an anti-freeze.

How can you tell a stoat from a weasel?

Stoats and weasels belong to the same family and look very similar. They both have reddish brown coats and white undersides. However, the stoat is usually larger than the weasel and always has a black tip to its tail.

How high can a flea jump?

Fleas have a spring mechanism in their bodies which enables them to fling themselves high in the air in much the same way as an arrow is released from a bent bow. A flea can jump 30 centimetres in the air, well over a hundred times its body length.

How tall is the tallest animal?

The giraffe is the tallest living animal, standing at nearly six metres to the top of its head.

How do camels avoid sinking in the sand?

A camel's feet are specially adapted for walking across deserts. Each foot consists of two large toes interconnected by skin, so that as the camel walks, its toes splay out, opening the web of skin between them. This large surface area prevents the camel's feet from sinking deeply into the sand.

How do toucans manage to fly with such large beaks?

For such a large, seemingly cumbersome structure, the toucan's beak is surprisingly light. This is because it is virtually hollow inside, except for the thin reinforcing cross struts which lend strength to the outer bony sheath.

How can you tell if an otter is in residence on a river bank?

Look for its droppings, or 'spraints' as they are known to naturalists. Otters mark out their territories by leaving their cigar-shaped spraints in prominent places along the river bank.

How did the Spectacled Caiman get its name?

The Spectacled Caiman is a relative of the alligator family, and may be found in the swamps of South America. It has a ridge between its eyes which looks like the bridge of a pair of spectacles – hence its name.

How far do Wandering Albatrosses wander?

Wandering Albatrosses have the longest wings of any bird, which equip them perfectly for their nomadic lifestyle. They glide and soar over the oceans of the southern hemisphere for days on end, travelling as far as 500 kilometres in a day. They come ashore only to breed.

How small is the Pygmy Marmoset?

The Pygmy Marmoset of the Amazon rainforest is the world's smallest monkey. It measures only 30 centimetres from its head to the tip of its tail.

How do moths communicate with each other?

Moths communicate using substances called *pheromones*. These are substances given off by the female to attract males and their presence is detected by the male's antennae. The antennae of some male moths are extremely sensitive. Some species can detect the presence of a female at distances of over three kilometres.

How many eggs can a queen bee lay in a day?

At the height of summer, a queen bee may lay as many as 1500 eggs a day – more than the weight of her own body. This number of eggs is necessary, as in a strong colony sometimes as many as 1500 workers die each day from exhaustion.

How do worker bees know when to prepare for a new queen?

A queen bee has glands near her mouth which secrete 'queen substance' which is licked off by the worker bees. As the queen grows older, she secretes less of this substance, which tells the workers to prepare cells for the new queen. Seasons are important: at the height of summer, when the hive is very crowded, the spread of queen substance becomes disrupted, and new queen cells are prepared.

How do Basilisk Lizards run across water without sinking?

The Basilisk Lizards of South America are among the few four-legged animals to run on two legs. Using their tails to help them balance, they can reach speeds of up to 12 kilometres per hour over short distances. They move so fast that they are able to skim across the surface of water for several metres without sinking.

How many species are there in the world?

No one knows the answer to this question. The vast majority of species are tiny insects and other invertebrates, most of which have never even been seen or given scientific names. Some estimates put the total number of species at over 30 million.

How far away can a widlebeest detect rain?

No one really knows, but some observers believe that they can respond to rainstorms as much as 50 kilometres away. Where there is rain there will soon be fresh green grass, so by migrating in the direction of rain, the wildebeest finds good food.

How fast can marlins swim?

At up to 80 kilometres per hour. Although not the fastest fish over short distances, marlins can sustain speeds like these for many hours. They are large fish, 3–4.5 metres (10–15 ft) long, with spiky fins, striped bodies and long pointed snouts.

How long can a parrot live?

Parrots are believed to have lived for over 70 years in captivity. In the wild they probably never reach this age, because they do not have their food provided for them as cagebirds do, and they would easily be caught by predators when old.

How do worm lizards tunnel through the earth?

Worm lizards, or *amphisbaenids*, are unusual reptiles that are not really lizards at all. Although they have no legs, they are not snakes either. They use their hard, chisel-shaped heads to burrow through the soil, twisting their bodes to push themselves forward.

How does a jellyfish sting?

With special stinging cells known as *nematocysts*. Rather like miniature fire extinguishers, the nematocysts can be used only once. They contain toxins which are injected by a long barbed tentacle. This tentacle is coiled up like a spring inside the nematocyst, ready to be released when needed.

How often does a mayfly feed?

Never. The adults live for only a few days at most, and do not feed at all. However the mayfly larva, a crawling, wingless animal that lives in water, does eat. It stores enough food in its body to keep the adult going during its short life.

How do bumble bees warm themselves up?

By shivering their muscles. The long soft hairs on their bodies help to keep the heat in.

How do Sea Otters stay together at night?

By wrapping strands of large seaweeds, known as kelps, around their bodies. The kelp keeps them together and prevents strong currents from sweeping them out to sea.

How does an animal's body fight disease?

Mainly with cells known as phagocytes, or 'eating cells', which can eat up bacteria and other microbes. Higher animals such as ourselves also have other defences, including antibodies, which help phagocytes to recognize their targets.

How can we see in colour?

By means of special light-sensitive cells in our eyes, known as cones. By responding to light of different wavelengths, they distinguish colours. We also have cells known as rods, that cannot see colours but are more sensitive to light overall.

How far can a kangaroo jump?

As much as 13 metres. This is about six times its own length, although when moving normally kangaroos only jump abour four times their own length.

How much can an elephant eat?

African elephants, which are larger than their Asiatic cousins, need about 150 kilograms of food in a day, but can eat about 350 kilograms if there is plenty of food available. Their diet is made up of leaves, bark and other plant food.

How was *Archaeopteryx* discovered?

The first fossil that was recognized as *Archaeopteryx* was found in 1861 by workmen in a limestone quarry in Germany. Other fossils had been found before then, but had been classified as ordinary dinosaurs, because the impression of the feathers was not present.

Index

ILLUSTRATORS
Graham Austin 4–9, 41–51
Bob Bampton 11–17
Norma Burgin 88, 89, 94, 95, 98, 99, 101, 111, 112, 117
Steve Crosby 52–61, 82, 90, 91, 107, 108, 110, 115, 118, 119
Steve Holden 120–133
David Holmes 62–77
Patricia Newell 78, 86, 87, 96, 97
Denys Ovendon 18–41
John Thompson 120, 133

PHOTOGRAPHIC ACKNOWLEDGEMENTS

The publishers wish to thank the following for supplying photographs for this book:

Page 5 Zambian Tourist Board; 12 Biofotos; 20 Biofotos; 21 Biofotos; 22 Michael Chinery *top* Pat Morris *bottom*; 23 N.H.P.A.; 26 Biofotos; 28 Nature Photographers; 30 Gene Cox; 31 N.H.P.A.; 38 Biofotos; 39 Pat Morris; 43 Biofotos; 46 R. Thompson *top* N.H.P.A. *bottom*; 47 Seaphoto; 50 N.H.P.A.; 53 Bruce Coleman; 60 Pat Morris; 61 N.H.P.A.; 64 Pat Morris; 65 Pat Morris; 71 Brian Hawkes; 72 N.H.P.A.; 78 G. R. Roberts; 81 A.N.I.B.; 89 Pat Morris; 90 Pat Morris; 92 Pat Morris; 94 Rao; 101 Pat Morris; 117 Bruce Coleman; 118 N.H.P.A.

Picture Research: Elaine Willis